THE CABANATUAN PRISON RAID

The Philippines 1945

GORDON L. ROTTMAN

First published in Great Britain in 2009 by Osprey Publishing,
Midland House, West Way, Botley, Oxford, OX2 0PH, UK
443 Park Avenue South, New York, NY 10016, USA
E-mail: info@ospreypublishing.com

Print ISBN 978 1 84603 399 5
PDF e-book ISBN 978 1 84908 4112 2

Page layout by: Bounford.com, Cambridge, UK
Index by Peter Finn
Typeset in Sabon
Maps by Bounford
3D BEV by Paul Kime
Originated by PPS Gramsmere Ltd, Leeds, UK
Printed in China through Worldprint

09 10 11 12 13   10 9 8 7 6 5 4 3 2 1

A CIP catalogue record for this book is available from the British Library

FOR A CATALOGUE OF ALL BOOKS PUBLISHED BY OSPREY MILITARY
AND AVIATION PLEASE CONTACT:

Osprey Direct, c/o Random House Distribution Center,
400 Hahn Road, Westminster, MD 21157
Email: uscustomerservice@ospreypublishing.com

Osprey Direct, The Book Service Ltd, Distribution Centre,
Colchester Road, Frating Green, Colchester, Essex, CO7 7DW
E-mail: customerservice@ospreypublishing.com

www.ospreypublishing.com

ACKNOWLEDGEMENTS

The author appreciates the information provided by Ike Suarez, Akira
"Taki" Takizawa, Pat Holscher, Steve Seale, and Carlo and Tonet Rivera.

ARTIST'S NOTE

Readers may care to note that the original paintings from which the
colour plates in this book were prepared are available for private sale.
All reproduction copyright whatsoever is retained by the Publishers.
All enquiries should be addressed to:

Howard Gerrard
11 Oaks Road
Tenterden
Kent
TN30 6RD
UK

The Publishers regret that they can enter into no correspondence upon
this matter.

THE WOODLAND TRUST

Osprey Publishing are supporting the Woodland Trust, the UK's leading
woodland conservation charity, by funding the dedication of trees.

EDITOR'S NOTE

For ease of comparison between types, Imperial/American measurements
are used almost exclusively throughout this book. The following data will
help in converting the Imperial/American measurements to metric:

1 mile = 1.6km

1lb = 0.45kg

1yd = 0.9m

1ft = 0.3m

1in = 2.54cm/25.4mm

1gal = 4.5 liters

1 ton (US) = 0.9 tonnes

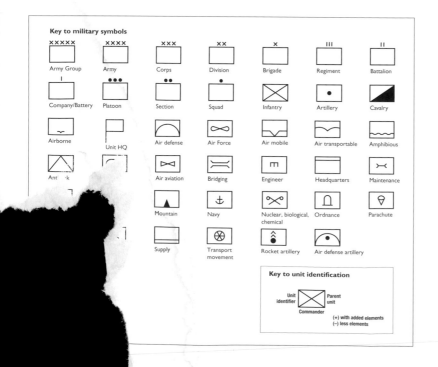

CONTENTS

INTRODUCTION

In the early hours of April 10, 1942 Japanese troops herded thousands of US and Filipino servicemen into columns on the southeast end of Bataan Peninsula near Mariveles. Other groups of prisoners were marched from Bagac on the far west side of central Bataan. They were about to begin what was to become the most notorious mass atrocity inflicted on US forces. The morning before, MajGen Edward P. King, Jr., commanding the Bataan Force, had surrendered 11,800 Americans, 66,000 Filipinos, and 1,000 Chinese-Filipinos to LtGen Homma Masaharu of the Japanese 14th Army. These men had been fighting ceaselessly for four months and for the last two had been on half rations or less. They were suffering from malnourishment, beriberi, extreme fatigue, malaria, and dysentery.

These troops, from a peacetime army, had never been taught how to conduct themselves in captivity and naively expected to be treated in accordance with the Geneva Convention. They had no idea what to expect and, with the short notice before their surrender, they had made no preparations.

The Japanese, regardless of assurances of humane treatment during surrender negotiations (one Japanese officer informed the Americans, "we are not barbarians"), were inadequately prepared for dealing with so many prisoners. They had expected the battle to continue and for many of the enemy to fight to the death as they would have done themselves. MajGen Kawane Yoshitake, transportation officer for the 14th Army, was given the task of planning the movement of the prisoners. He made preparations for only 25,000 detainees, not the eventual 79,000. Moreover, Japanese officers and soldiers had no idea of their obligations under the Geneva Convention and had been taught to despise Western protocols.

The Japanese "plan" was to move the thousands of already exhausted, starved, and ill prisoners north to Camp O'Donnell, a former Philippine Constabulary base with inadequate quarters and facilities. They unrealistically planned for the prisoners to carry their own rations and water. The problem was that virtually no rations remained, there was little to carry water in, and most US trucks had been disabled when the surrender was ordered.

What became known as the Bataan Death March threaded up Bataan's eastern coastal road through the sweltering jungle and sun-baked coastal plain. Surrendering troops had been formed up in scattered assembly areas and units broken up. Chains of command and unit cohesion disintegrated. Men were separated from their buddies and it soon became an every-man-for-himself situation. At different points some prisoners were given a can of food or a little rice. It is not known how many died by the end of that first horrible day. The exhausted prisoners slept in the open amid swarming mosquitoes and were driven to their feet at sunrise. Covering 10–15 miles a day, they were beaten northward to San Fernando, 63.4 miles from Mariveles. It was the dry season, but humidity was high and the temperature reached a scorching 104°F (40°C).

Besides these hardships, the brutalities inflicted on the men by their guards were horrendous and inexcusable. In addition to the lack food and water, no medical treatment was provided and the guards were often violent. Filipino civilians who tried to give prisoners food, water, and aid were driven off. Filthy water and even mud was lapped up from ditches and ruts by prisoners who soon suffered from stomach cramps and diarrhea. Prisoners falling out or unable to get to their feet after the rare breaks were shot or bayoneted on the spot, if not decapitated by sword-carrying officers and sergeants. Japanese troops aboard trucks passing the columns randomly bayonet-slashed and shot prisoners. Often, prisoners attempting to aid others were also killed. If a prisoner was found with Japanese money, mementos, or even items purchased before the war and marked "Made in Japan," it was assumed that these had been taken from Japanese dead and so the bearer was butchered. Prisoners died of their previous wounds, dehydration, heat exhaustion, starvation, and from illnesses contracted earlier. In their weakened condition few were able to slip away.

It took five or six tortuous days, depending on where prisoners started from, to reach San Fernando, the men arriving between April 12 and 24. Over that time the wounded and sick still in the hospital were forced out on the death road as they were considered "recovered" by their captors. There the men were packed in boxcars: 100 into baking hot, fully enclosed cars designed for 40. They traveled 30 miles to Capas with more dying during the four-hour ride. A 7-mile march to Camp O'Donnell followed. All the time they had no idea how far they were to travel, where they were going, or when the nightmare might end.

Some 9,200 Americans arrived at O'Donnell with an estimated 1,200–2,275 dying en route.[1] An estimated 42,800–50,000 Filipinos[2] made it to the camp, with about 9,000–14,000 perishing. Approximately 2,200 Americans and 27,000 Filipinos died in O'Donnell, where mass burials were daily occurrences and some prisoners even died digging their own graves.

APRIL 10 1942

Start of the Bataan Death March.

Some 79,000 American and Filipino troops were force-marched up the war-battered Bataan Peninsula for a torturous 64-mile nightmare. Thousands died owing to starvation, illness, fatigue, and outright murder. (US Army)

---

1 It must be noted the numbers of prisoners and their death rates vary widely between authorities. Seldom will two agree.
2 In July 1942 most Filipino prisoners were paroled, but many were simply transferred to labor units.

The Japanese had made virtually no preparations for the Death March, making little food and water available and not even permitting civilians to give it to the staggering prisoners. (US Army)

Contrary to popular perception, the prisoners captured in Corregidor did not take part in the Death March. Corregidor surrendered on May 6, 1942. On May 11, the 11,000 prisoners were loaded into three freighters bound for Manila. They were paraded through the streets to tout the Japanese victory, demonstrate America's weakness, and humiliate the prisoners. Crammed into the Old Bilibid Prison[3] near the dockyard for two or three days, they were taken by train to Cabanatuan City, and then marched to the Cabanatuan Prisoner of War Camp No. 1. Most US prisoners at O'Donnell were subsequently sent to the Cabanatuan camp, a former training facility of the 91st Philippine Division, between June and September 1942. Prior to serving as a military training camp, it had been a US Department of Agriculture research station dating from the 1920s. For a time it was the largest POW camp in the Philippines, housing 8,000 Americans. Within two months prisoners at O'Donnell began to be transferred to Cabanatuan as the former was gradually shut down. They endured a 7-mile march to Capas still in a weakened, if not a worse state than when they originally arrived. Packed once more into boxcars, they were railroaded to Cabanatuan City and marched 5 miles to the camp. Thousands of prisoners were subsequently sent from Cabanatuan to Japan, Manchuria, Formosa, Korea, and elsewhere in the Philippines as slave labor aboard the "hell ships." A final group of over a thousand was shipped off in December 1944 just before the Americans landed on Luzon.[4]

As prisoners departed for unknown fates, one incident encouraged those remaining at Cabanatuan, most of whom were too ill and disabled to travel, many being amputees. Long fearing they were forgotten, in the middle of the month, they witnessed an air battle over the camp, in which a Japanese fighter was shot down. They could not immediately recognize the aircraft or the markings as the US had changed its nationality identification after the Philippines fell, but, using Red Cross parcel playing cards showing Allied aircraft, they identified them as new Navy Hellcats – American aircraft carriers were nearby.

After the first stage of the march, and a railroad ride packed in boxcars, the surviving prisoners marched 7 more miles to Camp O'Donnell. Here prisoners carry those too weak to walk in single-pole litters. Filipino guerrillas used this same type of litter to carry weak prisoners from the Cabanatuan POW Camp three years later. (US Army)

---

3 This was the old national prison and now served as the Manila City Jail; not to be confused with the New Bilibid Prison opened in 1940 in southeast Manila near the shores of Laguna de Bay.

4 In December 2008 the Japanese government extended an apology through its ambassador in the US to former American prisoners of war who suffered in the Bataan Death March.

ORIGINS

The re-conquest of the Philippines commenced on September 18, 1944, when the 6th Ranger Battalion secured three small islands in the entrance to Leyte Gulf – the first mission for the untried unit. A vicious 3½-month battle for Leyte ensued. The next conquest was Mindoro, south of Luzon, on December 15. It was secured before the end of the month, allowing airfields to be built to support the assault on the main objective, Luzon.

The Luzon landing was conducted on January 9, 1945 – S-Day – in Lingayen Gulf on the west-central coast not far from where the Japanese had landed three years earlier. The 6th Ranger Battalion followed the main landing a day later. It was assigned only to secure Sixth Army HQ and to conduct patrols, and was held in reserve to employ on rapidly emerging special missions.

Two US corps had come ashore to drive southwest through the broad Agno/Pampanga River Valley to Manila 120 miles distant. I Corps, with the 43rd, 25th, and 6th Infantry Divisions, was on the east flank and heavily engaged with the Shobu Group in the foothills along the valley's north and northeast side. On the west flank, XIV Corps, with the 37th and 40th Infantry Divisions, was making good progress south toward the former Army Air Corps' base at Clark Field. About 12 miles north of the airbase was Camp O'Donnell. It would be liberated on January 30.[5] Gen Douglas MacArthur was placing much pressure on XIV Corps to take Clark Field as a base for fighter bombers, and then push on to Manila. In I Corps' sector the Japanese were funneling in more units, including elements of the 105th Division and 2nd Tank Division. Five battalions of the 105th Division were prepared to serve as a rearguard to cover the withdrawal of the Shobu Group northward.

The Japanese 14th Area Army had organized its forces into three groups. The largest was the Shobu Group, with 152,000 troops in four infantry divisions, a tank division, and an independent mixed brigade. It was responsible for the defense of northern Luzon and within the bounds of its southernmost area was Cabanatuan Camp. The 30,000-man Kembu Group was responsible for west-central Luzon and consisted of the 1st Raiding Group (a small airborne division) and regiments detached from Shobu Group divisions. Manila and all of southern Luzon was the responsibility of the Shimbu Group and its 80,000 men in two divisions. Gen Yamashita Tomoynuki, commanding the 14th Area Army, felt Luzon could not be held with the forces available. Even with the 2nd Tank Division he lacked the mobile forces to effectively defend such a large island – 40,800 square miles, about the area of the state of Virginia. He had lost two divisions and other units sent to defend Leyte. Little effort was made to defend the Agno/Pampanga River Valley as the Americans advanced toward Clark Field and Manila. American air attacks, coupled with increasingly bold guerrilla activity, forced Yamashita to move most units into the mountains to the north. Cabanatuan Prison Camp was located right in the middle of this battlefield.

Two days before the Luzon landing, on January 7, 1945, a US Army intelligence officer interviewed a former POW. Pfc Eugene Neilson had surrendered on Corregidor and eventually found himself in the Puerto Princesa POW Camp on Palawan, an island between Mindoro and Borneo. His story stunned the G2 (intelligence) officer. He had been among 150 prisoners constructing an airstrip under

---

5 Only a few US medical staff remained at O'Donnell, and it was being used as a Filipino labor camp.

**JANUARY 9
1945**

The Luzon landing.

brutal conditions. On December 14, 1944 they were ordered into air-raid shelters – long narrow trenches covered with logs and earth – drenched in gasoline, and set aflame. The guards shot down the smoldering men rushing from the tunnels and hunted down escapees, shooting, bayoneting, and even dousing them with gasoline and igniting them on the spot. Eleven prisoners, including Nielson, escaped to be found by guerrillas. Some of these men were evacuated by flying boat to Morotai Island in the Netherlands East Indies. Pfc Neilson's shocking report was forwarded to Sixth Army HQ on Luzon.

Sixth Army was already aware of the locations of POW and civilian internment camps on Luzon through guerrilla reports. LtGen Walter Krueger and his staff were familiar with the conditions in the camps, poor rations, inadequate medical care, beatings, and wrenched living conditions. It had been reported that the POWs were living on rice (often boiled down to a soupy starch called *lugao*), powdered fish, carabao[6] heads and intestines for soup, trapped rats and lizards, and the rare vegetables they could steal or barter.

Krueger's staff were also conscious of the complete disregard of the Geneva Convention by the Japanese, their willingness to sacrifice their own lives to destroy the enemy or prevent their own capture,[7] and the atrocities inflicted on prisoners elsewhere. Reports were coming in of the savage brutality meted out to Filipinos, while the recent report of the Palawan massacre only reinforced fears that the Japanese might murder prisoners about to be liberated. Palawan, while enduring an occasional air raid, had not even been invaded. Even the best-case scenario would spell doom for emaciated prisoners, namely that the Japanese would force-march them away from advancing US forces. There was little doubt that many would not survive the physical hardships of another death march. Even then there was a high probability of their eventual execution by their guards or a massacre by retreating Japanese troops. There was little hope of the Japanese guards simply abandoning them unharmed as Americans approached the camp. The figures were not known at the time, but only 4 percent of Allied prisoners of the Germans and Italians died in captivity, in contrast to 27 percent of those held by the Japanese.

The story of the Bataan Death March and other prisoner atrocities were also common knowledge in the rank and file. Escaped prisoners had linked up with guerrillas over the years. Some joined up and others were evacuated by submarine or flying boat to Australia. It was not long before articles were appearing in magazines and newspapers. Their story was well known and, to the soldiers liberating the Philippines, they were heroes.

---

6 Domesticated water buffaloes used as pack animals and for food.
7 Suicidal *banzai* charges and individual suicides to avoid capture had been an established fact since Guadalcanal. The first *kamikaze* (Divine Wind) attacks against ships commenced on October 25, 1944, during the battle of Leyte Gulf.

INITIAL STRATEGY

Early on January 26 an American wearing an old-style campaign hat appeared on horseback at Sixth Army HQ at Dagupan just inland from Lingayen Gulf. He had ridden 40 miles overnight, a hard cross-country ride under any circumstances, let alone through a war zone. Col Horton V. White, Sixth Army G2, received the rider. He was Maj Robert Lapham, a reserve officer originally assigned to the 45th Infantry (Philippine Scouts) as a second lieutenant. After the surrender of Bataan, Lapham formed a 10,000-man guerrilla group in central Luzon called Luzon Guerrilla Armed Forces (LGAF) or "Lapham's Raiders." This soft-spoken officer had a 1-million peso bounty on his head.[8] He had been part of a desperate 36-man mission striking out from Bataan with the aim of destroying Japanese aircraft at distant Clark Field. They had infiltrated almost to the field when they received word of the surrender. Rather than comply with the order, they went into the hills to form guerrilla bands.

Lapham was not unknown to the G2, which was familiar with his radioed reports long before the landing. He reported that his units had kept Cabanatuan POW Camp under surveillance. The camp was some 60 miles from Sixth Army HQ in Nueva Ecija Province. Nearby Cabanatuan City ("Place of the Rocks") was the province's capital. The camp's population fluctuated, but in past months many of the prisoners had been sent away, as the Japanese command had ordered that all POWs be evacuated from the Philippines to be employed as labor. Only about 500 remained and they were in bad shape. Lapham possessed details of the camp's layout, guard dispositions, and defenses. The guerrillas sensed that the guards would murder the prisoners en masse if their liberation appeared imminent. It was reasoned that as defeat appeared more apparent the guards would react suddenly and violently. But Lapham assured White that his guerrillas could assist in a rescue attempt.

A strange occurrence had taken place at the camp on January 6, three days before the American landing. Most of the guards hastily departed, leaving only a few ill men. The Japanese command was aware of the approach of the American invasion fleet and was forming ad hoc units. Virtually unguarded, the prisoners considered

A group of American and Filipino guerrilla leaders. Maj Robert Lapham is the third man from the left. Lapham was responsible for alerting Gen Krueger to the danger the Cabanatuan POWs were facing and coordinating the guerrilla support so essential to the mission's success. (US Army)

JANUARY 26 1945

Maj Robert Lapham arrives at Sixth Army HQ at Dagupan.

8 Lapham would later be presented with the Philippine Legion of Honor, becoming the third person to receive it after Franklin Roosevelt and Gen MacArthur, as well as the Distinguished Service Cross, the highest award for valor after the Medal of Honor.

LtGen Walter Krueger, Commanding General, Sixth Army. Krueger had the foresight to organize the 6th Ranger Battalion and the Alamo Scouts, which performed the Cabanatuan rescue. (US Army)

escaping, but half of them could not walk any distance. It was considered that a smaller, fitter group might escape, but it was feared that as they had no idea of the lie of the land beyond the camp, or the location of friendly forces, they would be swiftly hunted down. They were also reluctant to leave the helpless prisoners to the mercy of the guards. Understanding that there was a chance the guards might massacre them, they were making clubs and knives, determined that they would not go down without a fight. The guerrillas had no time to react, as over the next two days replacement guards trickled in. After the American landing on January 9, most of the guards again left, leaving just 20 to watch over the POWs. Nearing starvation, the prisoners took the chance of raiding the livestock pens right under the guards' noses. Slaughtering two carabaos, they served them out. After scrounging a great deal of the food the guards had left, the men were strengthened enough that if rescue came many could at least walk a short distance. Soon, additional guards arrived and a stricter regime was once again enforced.

After a meeting at 1500 hours, Col White, recognizing the volatility of the situation and the need to act quickly, notified Gen Krueger. Cabanatuan City was expected to be reached by I Corps in about five days – January 31 or February 1 at the latest. White estimated that if they did not make a rescue attempt by the 29th the prisoners were doomed or would be moved on foot, which could prove just as fatal. There was no time for a lengthy study of the situation, detailed planning and a leisurely decision. The decision would have to be made immediately and executed with all haste. The rescue force would have to infiltrate at least 30 miles of enemy territory. That alone would require two days. Extreme precautions had to be taken to ensure the rescuers were not detected, not only by the Japanese, but also by Filipino collaborators in villages who could inform on them. There were also communist People's Anti-Japanese Army (Hukbalahap or Huks) guerrillas in the area, who, although often fighting alongside US-supported guerrillas, were vehemently anti-American and could impede the progress of the raiders. If the Japanese were alerted they might move the prisoners or massacre them on the spot. They could also ambush the rescuers or launch an immediate counterattack as the would-be rescuers charged into the camp. Even more appalling would be the prospect of a successful liberation followed by a relentless pursuit, with the Japanese harassing a strung-out column of sick and frail men. No reaction force could respond quickly enough to save them if this occurred. Besides the camp guards, there were large numbers of troops from the 105th Division moving through the area, reinforced by tanks, although, for the most part, the Japanese stayed on the roads and did not actively patrol the countryside.

"Sounds risky," was Krueger's comment. The Texan general was indeed risking not only the lives of the prisoners and their rescuers, but his own reputation. The mission would have to be highly classified, with only select individuals informed of the final objective, to ensure any hope of success.

Krueger had to consider the motivations for the mission before making this crucial decision. Was it an emotional issue of rescuing the survivors of Bataan and Corregidor or was there a true military benefit? Krueger, having come up through the ranks, had a soft spot for the troops. Was it worth the risk of losing the rescue force and the prisoners? If anything went wrong there would be few survivors. There might also be retaliations against civilians and on villages en route if they were suspected of aiding the Americans. Did the risks justify the objective? Ultimately, Krueger felt the humanitarian mission warranted the risk. If successful, and his staff believed there was a 50/50 chance of it being so, it would have a great effect on morale among his troops and on the home front.

Some on the staff felt that the presence of Lapham's guerrillas improved the odds. They would provide guides and security, clear the way through villages, establish roadblocks to halt Japanese reinforcements and counterattacks, and assist the reconnaissance party that would first place the camp under surveillance. They would also provide unarmed auxiliaries to carry weakened prisoners by litter and carabao cart, as well as supplying food and water during the return to US lines.

In 1942 some of the fledgling guerrilla bands had attempted to conduct attacks on the Japanese, but, lacking adequate weapons, ammunition, supplies, training, command and control, and experience, they were often defeated. MacArthur ordered them to go to ground in order to preserve their forces, receive weapons, stockpile supplies, and train. Formal communication links and liaison teams were established between US forces and the guerrillas. Their most valuable role was to collect and report intelligence. Thanks to them, American forces were well informed on Japanese activities by the time they launched their assault on the Philippines. In September 1944 the guerrillas were finally given the orders they had long awaited – they were to actively attack Japanese lines of communications, destroying and harassing supply and troop movements.

Through 1944, Lapham's guerrillas proposed several times to raid the camp and release the 2,000 or so prisoners that were then held there. They would have to get

Capt Robert Prince, CO, Company C, 6th Ranger Battalion, chats with a Thompson .45cal M1 submachine gun-armed guerrilla after the raid. Initially uncertain of the abilities of the guerrillas, when it was all over the Americans held them in the highest regard. (US Army)

them to the east coast over 40 miles away across the open valley and then through the Sierra Madre Mountains – a most difficult task since the Japanese could devote their full resources to hunting them down. The Navy could not marshal the 20–30 submarines required to rescue the weakened and injured POWs. Any rescue attempt would have to wait until the Americans had landed and the invasion begun in earnest.

In September, Lapham's Squadron 201A chopped down and collapsed both the temporary and new permanent bridges the Japanese had built over the Cabu River just a mile east of the camp. The temporary bridge was on a spur 300 yards northwest of the highway, which had served as the main transport link in the area. It had been

LtCol HENRY A. MUCCI

Regardless of training and motivations, it takes an extraordinary leader to shape a unit into something special. "Hank" Mucci, born in Connecticut in 1909 to an Italian immigrant family, was raised with horses, his father being a horse-trader. He entered West Point Military Academy in 1932 and graduated 246th out of 276 in the Class of 1936. His love of horses – he had been in the Academy's equestrian team – led him to the Field Artillery, then still largely horse-drawn. He excelled in athletics and, while near the bottom of his class academically, he was known for his leadership and ability to inspire others. It is interesting to note that William Darby of the Rangers and Robert Frederick of the 1st Special Service Force were also artillerymen. Mucci's assignment at the time of the Pearl Harbor attack was as provost marshal of Honolulu, an experience where he no doubt learned much in regards to dealing with rough and ready soldiers, as well as earning his nickname: "Little MacArthur."

He took over command of the 98th Field Artillery Battalion on April 26, 1944, knowing it was to be converted to a Ranger battalion. Mucci demonstrated a great deal of skill molding his former artillerymen and volunteers from other units into a cohesive organization. He was known as a no-nonsense, tough-talking, charismatic, athletic, pipe-smoking disciplinarian who looked out for his men. He picked up a new nickname, "HAM" from his initials and his dramatic antics. As he led his battalion through training, many of the volunteers thought he was out to kill them. He was quick to anger and never hesitated to point out others' failings in a not-soon-forgotten manner. He was demanding, demeaning when he had to be, and offered praise when earned. He possessed a flinty sense of humor and, for all his flaring anger, was fair, making him highly regarded by the troops who both feared and admired him.

Less than two weeks after the raid, Mucci was promoted to colonel and given command of the 1st Infantry Regiment, 6th Infantry Division. Wounded, he retired in 1946. He ran for Congress that year, but was defeated. He became a representative for a Canadian oil company in Thailand. In 1974 a segment of Route 25 between Bridgeport, his hometown, and Newtown, Connecticut, was named the Col Henry A. Mucci Highway. Col Mucci died in Melbourne, Florida, on April 20, 1997. Among Col Mucci's decorations are the Distinguished Service Cross, Bronze Star, Purple Heart, and Combat Infantryman's Badge. He was inducted into the Ranger Hall of Fame in 1998.

1 The US Army Rangers who participated in the POW rescue traveled with the minimum of kit and equipment. This Ranger wears a typical fatigue uniform with white identification strip, M1944 combat boots, and a field cap. He carries two ammunition bandoliers (48 rounds in each), a first-aid pouch, a 1qt canteen (on the right hip) and a M1918 Mk 1 trench knife. He is armed with a .30cal M1 rifle.

2 The Cabanatuan POW camp sentries donned only minimal equipment when standing guard in the towers, fighting positions and at the gates. Many only wore one cartridge belt rather than the usual two. This camp guard is shown wearing the usual tropical uniform with field cap, puttees and boots. He carries a 30-round cartridge pouch, a canteen on his right hip and a Type 30 (1897) bayonet. He is armed with a Type 38 (1905) rifle.

Nellist Team of the Alamo
Scouts in 1944 prior
to the Cabanatuan raid.
(Left to right top row) Pfc
Galen Kittleson, Pfc Thomas
Siason, and Pfc Andy Smith.
(Left to right bottom row)
Pfc Wilbert Wismer and
1st Lt William Nellist.

constructed as the Japanese rebuilt the original 75ft bridge, which had been destroyed by retreating US-Filipino forces in 1941. A second new bridge was not completed until mid-November 1944, also requiring a new temporary bridge.

The next question facing Krueger was what unit he would select for this dangerous mission. Sixth Army's 47 infantry battalions had been fighting and marching for almost three weeks. They were far from exhausted, but combat was taking its toll. Additionally every unit was needed on the broad front and its flanks as they advanced south. The rescue force would have to cover 30 miles over moderately rough terrain, overrun a guarded camp, possibly fight off counterattacks, then march back with 500 weakened prisoners, and could well be engaged on the return. The 1st Cavalry Division (serving as dismounted infantry) was landing on Luzon the next day and could not possibly be ready on such short notice. The separate 503rd Parachute Infantry Regiment had just stood down after a grueling month-long fight on Mindoro. The 11th Airborne Division on Leyte was preparing for an amphibious and parachute assault on southern Luzon in five days. Fortunately, Krueger had foresight and had previously created two special units ideal for this mission.[9] He first considered other units, as he wished to preserve these special units for rapidly emerging critical missions. This was certainly the situation he now faced.

In November 1943 Krueger had directed the formation of a special reconnaissance training unit, the Alamo Scouts Training Center (ASTC) on New Guinea. It had a two-fold mission. First was to train selected individuals from Sixth Army infantry units in jungle and amphibious reconnaissance skills. Most would return to their units and pass on their skills. The six-week course taught physical conditioning, hand-to-hand combat, jungle survival, intelligence collection, scouting and patrolling, navigation, communications, Allied and enemy weapons, infiltration and exfiltration techniques, and rubber-boat handling. Candidates were required to have combat experience, be able to swim, be in excellent physical condition, and have 20/20 vision.

---

9 See Osprey Battle Orders 12: *US Special Warfare Units in the Pacific Theater 1941–45.*

Second, some graduates were selected for assignment to the Sixth Army Special Reconnaissance Unit – referred to simply as the Alamo Scouts.[10] Many were paratroopers or from the 1st Filipino Infantry Regiment, a US Army unit organized in the States. Uniquely, peer evaluation was used to select men for what can be called the US Army's first long-range reconnaissance patrol (LRRP) unit. Enlisted graduates listed the names of three enlisted men and three officers they would prefer to serve with on a team. Selected officers named the three enlisted men they desired on their team and the teams bore the names of each commanding officer. (Similar peer evaluation is used in today's Ranger Course.)

The Alamo Scouts operated in teams of one officer and between five and seven enlisted men, conducting covert scouting missions behind enemy lines. These were most often landing beach reconnaissance missions, but the Scouts also operated inland and occasionally snatched a prisoner for interrogation. The previous October, two teams, Rounsaville (six men) and Nellist (seven men) had liberated 78 Dutch, Javanese, and French civilian internees at Cape Oransbari, Netherlands New Guinea. The two teams were accompanied by a Dutch Army interpreter and three native guides, and were landed on the north side of the cape by PT boats, along with a four-man contact team that remained with the boats. The teams followed a 5-mile path through the jungle and at 0200 hours arrived at the inland village where the internees were held. The guides made contact with villagers and learned there were 25 Japanese soldiers plus five Kempeitai (military police) in another hut holding the village chief hostage. Two-and-a-half miles away, on the south side of the cape, was a Japanese beach outpost of four men with machine guns. A plan was quickly developed and the Scouts split into three groups to be in position before dawn. Rounsaville Team with two men from Nellist Team would attack the two Japanese groups in the village while the rest of Nellist Team hit the beach outpost. All three Japanese positions were struck by lightning-fast attacks and most of the enemy were killed in less than four minutes, with no friendly casualties. The internees were collected and led to the beach position where they were picked up by two PT boats at 0700 hours. The mission's success was credited to close team work, flexibility, and the ability to make quick decisions to meet the situation.

Having approved this operation, Col White contacted LtCol Frank Rawolle of the Sixth Army Special Intelligence Subsection which was responsible for the control of the Alamo Scouts and liaising with the guerrillas. Much to his delight, he found that both Nellist and Rounsaville Teams were available. Other Alamo Scout teams had already infiltrated into the Japanese rear area to conduct reconnaissance and contact cooperative guerrillas (not all guerrillas cooperated with US forces, some having their own political agendas). The Scout teams were organizing ammunition and supplies for the guerrillas, confirming their often inflated intelligence reports, and coordinating joint operations.

The muscle for the raid would come from another unit created by Krueger. Five Ranger battalions had operated in the Mediterranean and Europe, but none had been raised in the Pacific.

The 6th Ranger Infantry Battalion was of unusual origin. It began life as 2nd Battalion, 99th Field Artillery Regiment (75mm Howitzer, Pack) in July 1940. In January 1941 it was redesignated 98th Field Artillery Battalion (75mm Howitzer, Pack). After training in the mountains of Ft Carson, Colorado, it arrived in Australia in January 1943 for projected deployment on New Guinea. However,

---

10 Sixth Army's operating force was given the task force designation of ALAMO Force. Gen Krueger was from San Antonio, Texas, home of the Alamo.

Australian authorities would not allow its 800 mules ashore for fear of their carrying some disease dangerous to livestock. The following month the unit moved to New Guinea for a year's training. Even though there were still operations being conducted on New Guinea, there was no requirement for the mule-borne artillery battalion and, in April 1944, 33-year-old LtCol Henry A. Mucci was assigned as the battalion commander with the task of converting the unit to a Ranger battalion, as it was found that a pack howitzer battalion employed on Guadalcanal was more of a hindrance than a help. The mules and some of the artillerymen were shipped to Burma to serve with Merrill's Marauders and, later, the MARS Task Force in the opening of the Burma Road.

Of the 900 artillerymen in the battalion, only 300 enlisted men and 12 of the 31 officers volunteered for the Rangers. Over 200 additional men were selected from volunteers in replacement depots. The remaining gunners were a tough bunch. They had had to be able to handle the howitzers and deal with stubborn mules. They had a minimum height requirement of 5ft 10in and many were farm boys already familiar with the character of cantankerous animals. Magazine articles described the Rangers and former muleskinners as the biggest, toughest men in the army. Mucci drove the battalion hard, conducting 5-mile runs, 20-mile forced marches with full equipment, obstacle courses, organized athletics, swimming, weapons-handling, patrolling, small unit and raid tactics, and rubber boat training. He created a physically tough unit and emphasized flexibility. One of the most valuable doctrines he fostered was independent thinking on the part of leaders when operating on their own. Although the unit commenced Ranger training soon after Mucci took over, it was not redesignated the 6th Ranger Infantry Battalion until September 24, 1944. The unit kept a low profile and wore no insignia or rank. They referred to one another by nicknames in an effort to develop close-knit teamwork.

RANGER AND ALAMO SCOUT WEAPONS

The 6th Ranger Battalion was well armed with light infantry weapons. The .30cal M1 Garand rifle (8-round clip) was widely used. Some riflemen carried .30cal M1 carbines (15-round magazine) rather than rifles, as a degree of latitude was allowed, though most preferred the harder-hitting Garand. Riflemen carried 80 rounds in their cartridge belts plus two bandoliers, each with 48 clipped rounds. Those with carbines had at least five magazines, usually more. A few men, mostly NCOs, carried .45cal M1 or M1A1 Thompson submachine guns (30-round magazine). Many officers carried M1 rifles rather than carbines plus a .45cal M1911A1 Colt pistol (7-round magazine) as did medics, who also carried carbines or rifles. LtCol Mucci and the battalion surgeon only carried pistols. Some enlisted men carried back-up .45 pistols, as did the attached cameramen. Rather than the .30cal M1919A4 tripod-mounted machine guns called for in the table of organization and equipment, the machine gunners carried .30cal M1918A2 BARs (20-round magazine) with their bipods removed. Each platoon was authorized a 60mm M2 mortar, but they did not carry these as their weight and bulk, along with the ammunition, was too much for the distance traveled over rough terrain. They would also have been too dangerous to use to neutralize the camp guards owing to the proximity of the prisoners' quarters. The limited supply of ammunition would also have been of little use against a concerted counterattack. Each man carried two to four Mk IIA1 fragmentation grenades and many carried an M1918 Mk I or M3 trench knife, the former having integral brass knuckles. A few 2.36in M9 bazookas were carried along with some extras borrowed from the 6th Infantry Division for use against tanks. Some M1-armed riflemen carried M7 grenade launchers and M9A1 antitank rifle grenades to back up the bazookas. The Alamo Scouts were armed with a mix of M1 rifles and M1A1 folding stock carbines, a .45cal Thompson submachine gun, and all had an M1911A1 pistol, fragmentation and smoke grenades, and a trench knife.

Organizationally, the Ranger battalion was an odd unit, being modeled on a British Commando unit. A "Commando" was not only a member of a Commando unit, but a term describing both the unit's mission and size – for example, No. 4 Commando. It was equivalent to a battalion organized into six small troops. Standard 850-man US infantry battalions had a 120-man HQ company, three 190-man rifle companies, and a 160-man weapons company. A 514-man Ranger battalion paralleled a Commando in organization with only a 94-man HQ company, a 12-man medical detachment, and six 68-man Ranger companies (Companies A–F).

While a rifle company had a headquarters, a weapons platoon, and three 41-man rifle platoons, the Ranger company had only a four-man HQ and two 32-man platoons. Each of these small platoons were organized into a four-man HQ, two 11-man assault sections, and a six-man special weapons section, which could be armed with a 60mm mortar, a bazooka, or both as required. The assault sections had two five-man squads, each with a Browning automatic rifle (BAR).

The battalion's début mission was to secure three small islands at the entrance to Leyte Gulf for the mid-October 1944 first landing of the re-conquest of the Philippines. They installed beacon lights to guide the invasion fleet through the channel and raided a small Japanese installation to obtain intelligence. One company returned to one of the islands to wipe out the remaining Japanese. They reconnoitered other Leyte Gulf islands and secured Sixth Army HQ on Leyte.

The battalion landed on the second day of the January 1945 Luzon invasion. It was given no assignment, being held in readiness for special missions. In the meantime, it guarded Sixth Army HQ and conducted patrols where the Rangers saw some action. But Mucci was hoping that Headquarters would grant the Rangers a mission more suitable to their highly trained status, and, as yet, under-used skills.

Mucci was summoned to G2 on January 27 and briefed on the situation. This was exactly what his battalion had trained for.

THE PLAN

The Sixth Army Special Intelligence Subsection under LtCol Rawolle would conduct overall mission planning and coordination. The mission was planned with minimal need for external support. The 6th Infantry Division, which was in the frontline sector nearest to Cabanatuan, was tasked to provide transportation, rations, and medical support for 500 arriving personnel, but they had no idea as to who they would be and from where they were coming.

Rawolle quickly hammered out a simple plan immediately after his January 26 (Friday) meeting with Robert Lapham. He submitted it to Col White who briefed Gen Krueger and approved it after asking some questions. The Alamo Scouts would first infiltrate to place the camp under surveillance and make contact with the guerrillas who would play a major role in the raid. Even though Sixth Army had been ashore for less than three weeks, Rawolle was familiar with and had confidence in the guerrillas, especially after his meeting with Lapham. The Rangers would infiltrate cross-country, attack the camp, free the prisoners, and exfiltrate back to friendly lines. Guerrilla forces would block Japanese reinforcements and cover the withdrawal and exfiltration. Maj Lapham was disappointed not to be accompanying the Rangers, having been deemed more valuable coordinating guerrilla activities at the launch site.

The January 27 planning meeting at Sixth Army HQ was attended by the G2, Col White, LtCol Rawolle of the Special Intelligence Subsection, the guerrilla leader Maj Lapham, LtCol Mucci, and three Alamo Scout lieutenants: John M. Dove, William E. Nellist, and Thomas J. Rounsaville. All available information regarding the Japanese in the area, the camp's layout, the surrounding area's terrain, and the prisoners was examined and discussed. In order to maintain secrecy, Krueger had decided that the Army Air Force would not be told of the operation. P-61 Black Widow night fighters were on night patrols above the roads in search of Japanese troop columns and vehicles and would be ordered to stay away from the prison camp area on the night of the operation. Once the prisoners were liberated and on their way back, air cover would be available.

LtCol Mucci and his S1 (personnel officer), Capt Vaughn Moss, confer in the battalion's base camp. Moss did not participate in the raid. (US Army)

Radio silence would be maintained unless there was an emergency, such as engagement with the Japanese, attack by American aircraft, or the necessity to make last-minute changes to the plan. Radio communications would be accomplished by Morse code rather than voice transmissions. Transmitting at the radio's maximum range would result in garbled voice transmissions. They also decided not to use SCR-536 "handie-talkie" radios for intra-unit communications owing to the possible noise.

Mucci was concerned about the presence of Japanese tanks in the area. Besides the two tanks suspected to be in the camp, they were also reported passing on the road in small numbers. The major concern was the extent of troop traffic in front of the camp. Mucci was also worried about US patrols and outposts forward of US lines. This would be resolved through coordination with the 6th Infantry Division – on the return trip the Rangers would fire two green flares to identify themselves.

Lapham's value soon became apparent. Besides providing information on the camp and the Japanese, when the Rangers reached Lobong, his guerrillas there would escort them to the area near the camp where more guerrillas would join the force. Villagers would also provide food en route and assist the returning prisoners.

Lapham immediately began dispatching messengers to his commanders to begin preparations, underlining the word "RUSH" three times in his communications to emphasize urgency. One of his directives was to recover the antitank mines they had hidden away. He did not relay exactly what the mission would be, but there is little doubt that his guerrillas had an idea. The launch site would be the small road-junction town of Guimba approximately 18 miles northeast of Cabanatuan City. It was the southernmost position held by the 6th Infantry Division and had been secured in the early morning of January 26.

Alamo Scout 1st Lt John M. Dove, who had also planned and accompanied the Cape Oransbari rescue, would accompany the Rangers as liaison officer. The camp reconnaissance mission would be led by 1st Lt William E. Nellist, with 1st Lt Thomas J. Rounsaville as second-in-command. All three officers were close friends and had complete confidence in one another. Their men were experienced and competent, capable of accomplishing missions even if the rest of the team was destroyed. Two men in each team were Filipino-Americans. The 14 Alamo Scouts' part of the mission was to make contact with the local guerrillas, place the camp under surveillance, reconnoiter the surrounding area, and report intelligence and any changes in the situation.[11] After trucking to the Guimba launch site about 30 miles from Cabanatuan Camp they would move by foot to Balangkare (Balincarin in some sources) where the Cabu area guerrilla commander was headquartered. The route would avoid villages and roads as much as possible, as it was known that there was a great deal of Japanese traffic on the roads, especially at night. They would arrive at a point north of the camp the next morning, the 28th (Sunday), and in the afternoon would undertake the initial reconnaissance of the prison. There was little time for the Scouts to prepare, as they would soon be departing and moving all night.

The Rangers and Scouts were provided with maps and recent aerial photographs of the camp. It was noted that although the maps were printed in 1944, they were based on pre-war maps and comparing them to the aerial photographs showed that the wooded area across the road from the camp was now rice paddies. There were concerns that other data on the maps might be inaccurate, so they would have to

JANUARY 27
1945

**Sixth Army HQ
planning meeting.**

---

11 One of the Scouts, Pfc (later Command SgtMaj) Galen Kittleson, had an extraordinary record of participation in military raids to free POWs. He took part in the Oransbari and Cabanatuan rescues in Nellist Team. As a Special Forces NCO he participated in the unsuccessful 1968 attempt to rescue Maj Nick Rowe held by the Viet Cong. In 1970 he took part in the Son Tay Prison Camp raid into North Vietnam.

rely on the guerrilla guides instead. The meeting broke up and the Ranger, Scout, and guerrilla officers rushed off with much to do.

On the afternoon of the 28th the Rangers would be trucked to Guimba and then move on foot following a slightly different route than the Scouts to Balangkare, arriving in the early morning of the 29th (Monday). Scout representatives would meet them and pass on updated information. Briefed by Col White, LtCol Rawolle, and Maj Lapham, Mucci was designated the overall commander on the ground and would make any necessary adjustments to the plan. The raid was tentatively planned for that night. Mucci had the freedom to postpone the raid to await a better situation or cancel it altogether if there were too many Japanese in the area. It was known that large numbers were moving through the area and that the central portion of the camp was being used as a rest site for units in transit. This not only provided shelter and reinforced the camp in the event of guerrilla attacks, but also protected them from air attack, even though shielding combat troops by hiding in close proximity to POWs was illegal. A larger bivouac was established on the north side of the road one mile east of the camp in a thicket on the Caba River. National Highway 20 passed directly in front of the camp, connecting with National Highway 5 at Cabanatuan City to the west, and leading north to the frontlines and south to Manila. Highway 5 was also important because it ran north of San Jose and was a main escape route into the Cordillera Mountains of north-central Luzon. The Japanese plan was for the 152,000-man Shobu Group to conduct a fighting withdrawal into the mountains and fight the Americans on favorable ground.

Any adjustment to plans made at Balangkare on the 29th was not final either. Changes could be made as necessary up to the last minute before execution. This degree of flexibility, and the ability to coordinate rapidly so that all elements were aware of changes, would be a major contributor to the success of the raid. It is essential for the execution of any successful raid or operation. Often in planning there comes a time when eleventh-hour "good ideas" become a potentially fatal hindrance. However, in many operations, especially special operations, last-minute changes are frequently necessary. The enemy is uncooperative and their actions and changes in procedures or routine cannot be foreseen. One cannot base a plan on what one expects or wishes the enemy to do. This was often a flaw in Japanese planning which was far less flexible than that of their opponents.

The Ranger and Alamo Scout plans changed throughout the operation with frequent fine tuning. Imagination was encouraged and this resulted in innovative ideas that reinforced the success of the bold and audacious plan. While the Japanese were concerned with an attack by local "bandits" (hizoku) – the name they gave to guerrillas (some of whom actually were bandits) – they did not expect an American strike force to appear out of the darkness in a lightning-swift attack. It is doubtful that the Japanese were even aware of the existence of the 6th Ranger Battalion or the Alamo Scouts. Their contempt for POWs may also have deluded them into thinking the Americans would not bother to mount a rescue. To the Japanese mind, they would have been of no further use as combat soldiers owing to their sick and weakened conditions and, furthermore, they had proved themselves unworthy and dishonorable by surrendering. The Japanese called stragglers and unarmed soldiers yuhei – "useless troops."

The most dangerous part of the operation was the withdrawal and exfiltration. Unless the opposition is wiped out or so thoroughly neutralized that it cannot undertake a pursuit, the disengagement from a raid can be the most risky phase. Counterattack by an external force and pursuit by a superior force are also major dangers. This raid would require a long-distance, overland exfiltration, much of it across open country. It would be complicated by the presence of over 500 sick, disabled and, most likely, disoriented former prisoners – on foot, weak, unarmed, and unorganized. They would be scattered and slaughtered if the Japanese were to attack.

It was planned for the guerrillas to cover the withdrawal and block Japanese reinforcements, but even though there was a degree of trust placed in them, they were an unknown quantity. Although they had been harassing the Japanese and were experts at hit-and-run tactics, they had not taken part in stand-up battles. It was not known how they would fare when facing determined Japanese frontal attacks and possibly tanks. Additionally, there was no accurate information on the locations and strength of Japanese units in the area. They were continuously arriving and departing, so only rough estimates were available. There was no telling if a large force might move through the immediate vicinity at the wrong time. Nor were there any realistic estimates on exactly how the Japanese would respond to the raid. Would they pursue with a modest or large force? Would it be a simple pursuit or would they move units from different directions to cut off or envelope the vulnerable column? Would they even do anything proactive other than continue to deploy troops in support of their withdrawal plan? They might not let the raid distract them from their main effort. The guerrillas feared the Japanese might content themselves with inflicting retribution on civilians in the area. Once they had covered the raiders' and prisoners' withdrawal they would need to concern themselves with that threat.

The Rangers mount out

With a flexible plan in hand, Mucci returned to his unit on the afternoon of the 27th. He had been closeted away with the G2 people all morning, hammering out the plan and completing it by noon. He would not need the entire battalion: Companies B and E were guarding a radar site on Santiago Island anyway. Company C was selected for the Cabanatuan mission. It had fought on Dinagat Island in Leyte Gulf and performed very well. Since Ranger companies were so small it was reinforced by 2nd Platoon, Company F. Charlie Company was commanded by a non-career Reserve officer, 23-year-old Capt Robert W. Prince. As a citizen soldier, he was not looking for rash but career-making opportunities, wanting little more than to finish the war and go home to his wife, and he was generally regarded as less prone to dramatics than his superior Mucci. He was considered optimistic, demonstrated good judgment of people and circumstances, was an advanced thinker, and, most importantly, was cool and rock-steady. Mucci himself thought highly of Prince and no doubt Charlie Company was selected based more on Prince's abilities than on an overall assessment of the company. But Prince had a problem he concealed from Mucci. His feet had not recovered from jungle rot and the beating they had taken in the long months of training on New Guinea. It had been three months and they still had not healed. Service on perpetually wet Leyte in the meantime had not helped his condition. He had a 60-mile walk ahead of him. Optimism was a good trait to possess considering the condition of his "dogs." Nonetheless, standing down from the mission was not an option Prince considered.

While Mucci was the "mission commander," he had the good judgment and confidence to name Prince as the "assault commander," with Prince ably assisted by his first sergeant – 26-year-old Charles S. Brosard. It was an excellent command decision. The overall mission commander should never lead the assault: there are too many other elements and issues for him to be concerned with. He needs to remain sufficiently distant to be able to absorb the local "big picture" of the immediate operation, make decisions, and control and coordinate all other elements, no matter how minor. He cannot do this if focused on the execution of the assault.

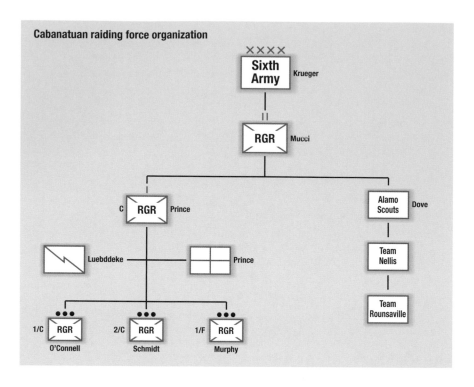

Cabanatuan raiding force organization

The waiting Rangers knew something important was in the works. A meeting was called and Charlie Company fell in with 2nd Platoon, Fox Company, and a few other selected individuals. Mucci informed the expectant men that the mission would be dangerous and some might not return. He suggested that married men and anyone harboring doubts withdraw. His remarks deterred no one: this is what they had signed up for and would be a test of their arduous training. Mucci only briefed them on the barest details of the plan. More solid information would be forthcoming. They would be taken by truck to a launch site in the morning, walk 30 miles cross-country, liberate over 500 prisoners from Bataan and Corregidor, and bring them home, "even if you have to carry them on your backs." At the end he informed them that there would be church services in 30 minutes and that he expected each man to get down on his knees and "swear that you'll die fighting rather than let any harm come to those prisoners." "Dammit, don't fake it!" he demanded. Every man attended church call.

Besides the reinforced company, other small elements participated. A four-man communications element was provided by the HQ Company. There was also a four-man medical element headed by the battalion surgeon from the Medical Detachment. Capt Robert W. Fisher was a Harvard Medical School graduate and popular among the troops for the care he lavished on them. The surgeon had to convince Mucci to let him go. He was too valuable to risk losing, but the prisoners and any severely wounded might need him. After word of the mission spread a couple of dozen men from other companies attempted to persuade Mucci to take them. Most he turned away, but some managed to sway him, including the Company A and F first sergeants, and an NCO each from Companies E and F. Even Mucci's executive officer, Maj Robert W. Garrett, tried to convince his CO to send him instead of the colonel, who, he claimed, was too valuable to the battalion. No doubt that was a short conversation.

In total, there were 121 Rangers plus a mascot spider monkey belonging to a Company F Ranger. Attached to record the event for posterity were a lieutenant and three enlisted men from Combat Photography Unit F, 852nd Signal Service Battalion. It was Mucci's idea to take the still- and motion-picture cameramen. After all, these men had seen more combat than the Rangers.

The enemy

The 105th Division under LtGen Yoshitake Tsuda[12] was a newly raised formation created in the Philippines in June 1944. It was organized from the six-battalion 33rd Independent Mixed Brigade and additional personnel sent from Japan. The 33rd itself had been raised in the Philippines in late 1943. The division was what was called a "brigaded division," as, rather than consisting of three three-battalion infantry regiments and an artillery regiment, it was organized into two brigades, the 81st and 82nd Infantry Brigades, each with four independent infantry battalions. Other divisional elements were the battalion-sized Artillery, Engineer, Signals, and Transport units. Its authorized strength was 13,000 troops and, at this point, its casualties had been relatively light.

The 105th Division was moving north to join the Shobu Group. Some units would stay behind as rearguards. As units passed north through Cabanatuan City, battalions were tasked to defend San Jose 25 miles to the north and Bongabon 20 miles to the east. One of the battalions assigned to this mission was the 800-man 359th Independent Infantry Battalion of the 82nd Brigade. Capt Oyanu Tomie's battalion was resting at Sangitan on the east edge of Cabanatuan City which they had passed through on their way from the south, and he was anticipating orders to proceed to either San Jose or Bongabon – a route that led past the Cabanatuan POW Camp. In the afternoon he was ordered to march to San Jose that night.

Reaching San Jose on the morning of the 26th, the battalion prepared to defend the town. But in the late afternoon of the 27th, they received orders to return to Cabanatuan City. However, because of the American advance the battalion would have to march 22 miles to the southeast to Bongabon on the night of the 29th and then 20 miles to Cabanatuan City on the

CABANATUAN RAID LEADERSHIP

Raid Commander	LtCol Henry A. Mucci
Company C	Capt Robert W. Prince
1st Sergeant	1st Sgt Charles H. Bosard
1st Platoon, Company C	1st Lt William J. O'Connell
1st Aslt Section	SSgt Preston N. Jensen
2nd Aslt Section	Sgt Homer E. Britzius
Spl Weapons Section	SSgt Manton P. Stewart
2nd Platoon, Company C	1st Lt Melville H. Schmidt
1st Aslt Section	SSgt Clifton R. Harris
2nd Aslt Section	SSgt William R. Butler
Spl Weapons Section	SSgt August T. Stern, Jr.
2nd Platoon, Company F	1st Lt John F. Murphy
1st Aslt Section	SSgt Richard A. Moore
2nd Aslt Section	SSgt David M. Hey
Spl Weapons Section	SSgt James O. White
Communications Element	1st Lt Clifford K. Smith
Medical Element	Capt James C. Fisher
Combat Photo Unit F (-)	1st Lt John W. Luebddeke
Sixth Army Spl Recon Unit (Alamo Scouts)	
Liaison	1st Lt John M. Dove
Nellist Team	1st Lt William E. Nellist
Rounsaville Team	1st Lt Thomas J. Rounsaville

---

12 Listed incorrectly as "Gen Naotake" in most sources, due to faulty intelligence information.

night of the 30th. The battalion commander felt it was too late that day to depart San Jose. He proposed that his unit march through Bongabon on the next night, the 29th. On the night of the 30th they would march to the Cabanatuan POW Camp, bivouac there through the day, and then march into Cabanatuan City in a couple of hours on the evening of the 31st. The proposal was partly rejected as the Kinpeidan HQ Unit would be resting at the camp. Oyanu's battalion was directed to march to the Cabu River bridge by the morning of the 30th and bivouac on the east side of the river. The headquarters unit would depart the camp at 2000 hours on the evening of the 30th, heading for Bongabon, and once there they would clear the bridge as they marched east. The 359th Battalion would then march west past the camp.

The troops were well armed with Arisaka rifles, Nambu light and heavy machine guns,[13] 5cm grenade dischargers ("knee mortars"), and hand grenades. They were outfitted in lightweight tropical uniforms of dark green, field caps, and steel helmets.

The Kinpeidan HQ Unit,[14] about 175 men, had marched or been driven in two trucks to the POW Camp from Cabanatuan City in the late afternoon of the 27th. They would remain there in the central compound until departing on the 30th. They were not involved with guarding the prisoners, but did post their own sentries.

On the 28th, the situation was deteriorating for the 105th Division. The Americans were pressing closer to San Jose and Cabanatuan City, but the units tasked to defend them were arriving too slowly. Fearing that the Americans might strike as soon as February 1 or 2, LtGen Yoshitake was trying to assemble a force of 6,000 troops. Only three battalions were in position in Cabanatuan City: two on the west side and one on the north, which needed to be reinforced. Yoshitake needed the 359th Battalion for that purpose and it was en route, but needed to arrive before midnight on the 30th. He also ordered the 2nd Shusei Battalion[15] in San Jose to move to Cabanatuan City following the same roundabout route as the 359th, but it was unrealistic to expect it to arrive in time.

Little was known about the 75 guards at the camp. Most were new to the assignment, having trickled in over several days after January 9, after most of the original guards were called away a few days earlier. It is not known if they were detailed from an infantry unit or if they were line-of-communications or other service troops. Often prison camp guards were Koreans, Formosans, and Okinawans, considered second-class soldiers by the Japanese. The Koreans were particularity noted for their brutality to prisoners.

Terrain and weather

The eastern end of the Agno/Pampanga River Valley, some 120ft above sea level, was flat and mostly open, although there were areas covered with bamboo, brush, and forests. The open areas were grassland, pastures, and rice paddies. Several narrow and shallow rivers meandered southward to merge into the Pampanga River just north of Cabanatuan City and continued south, passing the city on its west side. The Rangers would cross these rivers, but they were no more than broad, shallow streams and posed no obstacle in the dry season. The northward-flowing Cabu River was just over one mile east of the camp and flowed into the Pampanga River north of Cabu. It served as an obstacle to tanks and, to a lesser extent, infantry, not so much because of the water, but because of the depth of its steeply banked ravine. The Cabu River

---

13 It is not known whether the rifles and machine guns were 6.5mm or 7.7mm weapons.
14 This was the Kempeitai (military police) HQ of the 14th Area Army.
15 This unit is referred to as the Inoue Battalion (after the commander) in references. *Shusei* means "collect" – an ad hoc unit assembled from miscellaneous troops.

and the area around the village were wooded on both banks, although the density of the vegetation in the area was no real obstacle. The major impediments to cross-country foot movement were the rice paddies. Both the dried and still wet and muddy paddies were difficult to walk through, slowing movement rates. Coupled with the stream and river crossings, the wet rice paddies ensured continuously wet feet, which caused blisters. Numerous small *barrios* (villages) were scattered through the area. These were simply small collections of traditional Filipino-style houses built of local materials and known as *bahay-kubo* (nipa huts).

The dry season provided an afternoon high of 90°F (33°C) or slightly higher, while at night the temperature dropped into the low 70°F (20°C) range. High daytime humidity was about 97 percent and in the mid-50 percent range at night. There was no rain and very little or no breeze to give any relief from the heat. In the late afternoon a gusty breeze lasted for a couple of hours. Overall it was hot and humid, and the ground was parched. The skies were mostly clear with occasional spotty, drifting clouds.

Sunrise on January 30, the day of the raid, was 0629 hours, but there was enough light by 0606 hours – beginning of morning civil twilight – to conduct military operations without difficulty. Sunset on January 30, the night the raid occurred, was at 1751 hours and end of evening civil twilight (sun 6° below the horizon or about 20 minutes after sunset, still with sufficient light to see short distances) was at 1815 hours. Moonlight was a major concern. There would be a near-full moon, specifically a waning gibbous, with 96 percent of the moon's disk visible, rising at 1938 hours. That meant that there was only just over an hour of complete darkness between the sun sinking below the horizon and the moon rising. After rising, the moon would be low and cast long shadows to hide in, but it also provided the guards with fair visibility across the bare ground around the camp. The moon would set at 0829 hours the next morning, after sunrise.

The terrain around the camp was level and open. The Japanese kept the vegetation cut short, to detect both escapees and approaching guerrillas. National Highway 20 ran from Cabanatuan City north-northeastward in front of the camp, crossed the Cabu River on a 75ft long, 21ft wide timber bridge, and ran on to Bongabon.

The objective – Cabanatuan Prisoner of War Camp No. 1

Cabanatuan POW Camp No. 1[16] was located on the south side of the east–west road connecting Cabanatuan City and Bongabon – National Highway 20 – a two-lane asphalt road riddled with potholes. The camp was beside Pangatian, a small barrio about 5 miles east of Cabanatuan City and with Bongabon 10 miles to the northeast. Another barrio, Cabu, was 1 mile to the east of the camp on the west side of its namesake river. The camp was also known as Camp Pangatian because Pangatian barrio was the closest village. In fact, at the time of the raid, "Pangatian" appears to have been more used by the raiders than "Cabanatuan." Cabanatuan City, however, had a population of 50,000 and was the provincial capital, and was thus more recognizable.

The camp's barracks and other buildings were traditional nipa huts. They were 60ft long, 20ft wide, and made of split bamboo sides, bamboo framing, and nipa palm thatch roofs. The length of the sides was open halfway up the walls and fitted with top-hinged shutters. This helped air circulation, but did not keep out the swarms of mosquitoes and flies. The buildings were 2–3ft off the ground and the floors made of split bamboo or planks, each with a double-wide door at one end. The barracks

---

16 Camps No. 2 and 3 had been in warehouse complexes in the general area and were no longer used.

had a double-decked row of bamboo sleeping platforms down each side. There were many additional buildings, chiefly in the motor pool area, where there were two corrugated steel-roofed and sided sheds housing the two to four suspected tanks. These tanks may well have broken down and been left there to be repaired later. There were about 130 headquarters, supply rooms, barracks, sheds, kitchens, hospital wards, and other buildings plus about 70 small outbuildings, latrines, and washrooms, many of which had been added upon the camp's conversion to a military training camp. The only masonry building was a small chapel beside a pond not far from the front gate. Small-arms fire could riddle all other buildings in the camp.

Surrounded by three 8ft-high barbed-wire fences 4ft apart, the 600x800-yard rectangular camp was subdivided into three sections north to south by 6ft-high barbed-wire fences. Its long axis ran north-northwest to south-southeast. The northern half of the easternmost section was fenced across its south end. This 180x230-yard section was the actual POW compound and contained about 60 buildings. The modest medical area was in the south end. The guards' quarters were opposite this in the central sector with the officers' quarters, support facilities, communications center with power generator (for radios and lights in the Japanese

The internal layout of Cabanatuan Prisoner of War Camp No. 1.

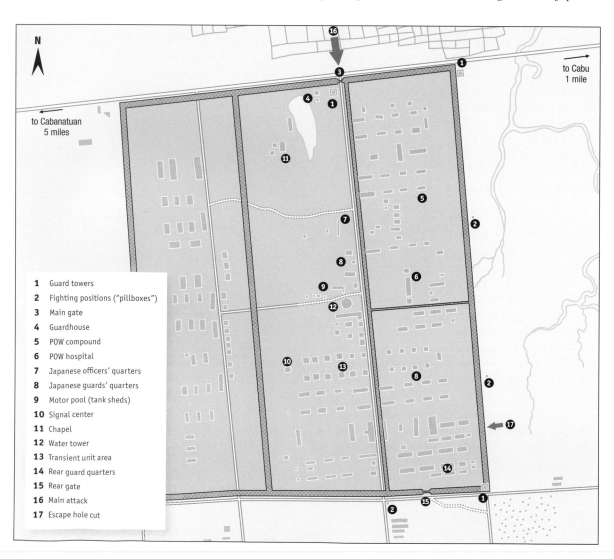

N

to Cabanatuan
5 miles

to Cabu
1 mile

1 Guard towers
2 Fighting positions ("pillboxes")
3 Main gate
4 Guardhouse
5 POW compound
6 POW hospital
7 Japanese officers' quarters
8 Japanese guards' quarters
9 Motor pool (tank sheds)
10 Signal center
11 Chapel
12 Water tower
13 Transient unit area
14 Rear guard quarters
15 Rear gate
16 Main attack
17 Escape hole cut

A prisoner's wartime sketch of the interior of a POW camp barracks. A row of double-pier bamboo sleeping platforms ran down either side of the barracks. The center aisle was planked while the floor under the bunks was split bamboo. (US Army)

section), motor pool, and transient unit quarters. More guards' quarters were in the south end of the eastern sector, while the western section was unused. An H-pattern dirt street system spanned the camp with two streets running its length north to south (connected by an east to west cross-street). The easternmost street edged the prisoner compound. The north end of this street connected to the Cabanatuan–Bongabon Road (National Highway 20) and served as the main gate. Civilians traveled the road and this allowed guerrillas to send people to check on the camp, note details, and barter with the guards who would buy food from them. Even children played games with the gate guards as part of this reconnaissance.

Besides enclosing the prisoners, the camp had to be secured from guerrilla attack. In fact the original guard detail's main task was more oriented toward thwarting an attempt by guerrillas to free the prisoners than preventing weakened prisoners from escaping. Three 12ft-tall guard towers with nipa thatched roofs for protection from the sun were erected at the camp's main gate (northwest corner of the prisoner compound, northeast corner, and southeast corner). There was a rear gate near the southeast corner. There were also three so-called "pillboxes" protecting the camp. These were actually open-topped fighting positions with built-up parapets. Though this is not confirmed, they probably had nipa roofs for sun protection, but none of the heavy protective overhead cover and narrow firing ports normally associated with pillboxes. Two were located on the east side of the camp, one outside the prisoner compound, one outside the guards' area and the third at the southwest corner on the easternmost section near the rear gate. Typically, four guards manned each tower and the fighting positions were equipped with rifles and a light machine gun. There were no searchlights, but this was not known by the raiders. Zigzag trenches intended for camp defense and as air raid shelters had been dug around the outer buildings on the west-central side and southwest corner of the guard compound. Guards also manned the front and rear gates, patrolled the camp's perimeter, and roved throughout the camp, although it appeared that no external security patrols were conducted. Running roughly parallel with the east fence was a meandering stream 2ft deep at its south end and 6ft where it crossed under National Highway 20. On the north side of the highway across from the camp the ground was covered with rice paddies, while the camp cemetery was outside the southeast corner.

THE RAID

The Alamo Scouts infiltrate

The Alamo Scout teams were trucked from Sixth Army HQ, departing at 1400 hours on the afternoon of January 27, to the barrio of Guimba, an almost 80-mile trip. Located in central Nueva Ecija Province, Guimba was in the middle of rice-growing country and marked the southernmost point of the American advance in the I Corps zone. While elements of the 6th Infantry Division's 1st Infantry Regiment were dug-in outside the barrio, they were not immediately faced by any Japanese, though many of the town's few thousand population had fled. They had occupied the barrio on the morning of the 26th.

Upon arrival in the afternoon, the Scouts loaded up with ammunition and rations, received radio frequencies and call signs, and departed in the late afternoon with a guerrilla, Sgt Pacifico Tuallo. They moved out following a slightly different route than the one the Rangers would follow the next day.[17] Accompanied by guerrilla guides, the small party made good time. The two Scout teams arrived at Balangkare and, from there, went to Platero a mile north of the camp and then on to the camp itself.

At 0500 hours on January 28, the Rangers loaded up in 2½-ton trucks at their bivouac outside Calasio on the south end of Lingayen Bay. They made the 2-mile trip to Dagupan, where the Sixth Army HQ sat astride the I and XIV Corps boundaries. It was a brief stop to draw bazookas and HEAT rockets, and to pick up the four cameramen. Fifteen minutes after arriving, the convoy departed and drove southwest. The roads were dense with two-way traffic and American planes crowded the skies. Smoke columns from burning villages and bombing attacks could be seen to the southeast and north.

The convoy pulled into Guimba at about 0715 hours and the Rangers assembled in a mango grove. About 8 miles to the east-southeast was Baloc. Baloc was a road junction with National Highway 20 running from Cabanatuan City in the south to San Jose in the north. The highway was under Japanese control. Here, Maj Lapham introduced Mucci to Capt Eduardo Joson, the guerrilla leader whose Squadron 213 was awaiting their arrival in Lobong 6 miles to the east-southeast. The Rangers checked their weapons, ammunition, and equipment. They traveled light without backpacks, typically carrying a 1qt canteen, cartridge belt, one or two bandoliers of ammunition, two to four grenades, first-aid pouch, and a knife. Some carried musset bags or ammunition bags for spare gear and grenades. Their loose-fitting faded green fatigues bore no insignia, and they wore well-broken-in brown leather combat boots, the new type with two-buckle strap uppers eliminating the need for leggings. Although the Rangers had worn helmets during previous operations, they left them behind for now, instead wearing field caps because helmets restricted vision and hearing, offered a distinctive silhouette, and noisy if accidentally struck. Everyone removed rings to prevent reflections. Medics were loaded with all the medical supplies and plasma bottles they could bear. The 2.36in bazooka rockets were distributed between the men and the launcher tubes broken down into two sections for carrying.

Each man drew nine small K-ration meals plus a stack of Hershey chocolate bars to share amongst the freed prisoners, carried in fatigue cargo pockets. It did not occurred to the Rangers that the prisoners had never seen K-rations, these having

---

[17] Unfortunately no map of the Scouts' route exists.

been standardized after the fall of the Philippines. The Rangers were served a hot lunch and made final preparations to depart. They drank their fill of water, topped off canteens, and checked their gear and weapons to ensure they made no noise. Most caught some sleep, in anticipation of having no further opportunity to do so until after they returned, up to 48 hours later.

The Ranger approach march

At 1400 hours, Mucci passed the word and without fanfare the column began its 30-mile march, striking out on a dirt road to the east. After 2 miles they reached a barrio named Consuelo and, from there, turned south across dry grasslands. The single-file column was kept tight, being stretched out to just over 100 yards with the men at close intervals. Two young guerrilla guides were at the head of the column with Mucci, Prince, and Dove. Mucci, though, roved up and down the column checking on his Rangers and encouraging them. They moved fast even though it was the hottest part of the afternoon. It began as any other of the many forced marches the Rangers had undertaken in training. Oddly, a single Ranger radio operator in a Dodge command car mounting an SCR-284 radio was parked at a point 1 mile southeast of Guimba. Sgt James M. Irvine would have to remain awake, monitoring the radio alone, for the mission's entire duration. This would be the main relay site between the raiders and Sixth Army. Another relay site was established 9 miles south of Guimba at Licab. Five men on foot would man it with a portable SCR-694 radio. In addition, the raiders carried another SCR-694.

The perils of the trek were many: ambush by Japanese or anti-American guerrillas, being informed on by collaborator villagers, or a chance encounter with a Japanese patrol. Other risks, and perhaps more likely, were a chance US artillery barrage landing on them or a mistaken attack by their own fighters. It was a serious concern that they might be attacked by friendly aircraft so far out beyond their own lines and heading deeper into enemy territory. Admittedly, there was little danger of the column running into a Japanese patrol. They had learned from the guerrillas that the Japanese seldom ventured into the countryside, staying on the roads and in the towns and not even patrolling beyond sight of roads.

The grasslands soon turned into rice paddies. The harvest had taken place the month before, much of which went to feed the Japanese occupiers. The refusal of Filipinos to deliver food quotas, as well as sabotage and passive resistance had increased after word of the Leyte landing spread. The going became difficult as many of the paddies were muddy or still contained some water over the inches of deep mud. The dry paddies were even more difficult, as countless carabao tracks had dried in the mud, creating ankle-twisting pockmarks. The small earth dikes were too dry and crumbled if one walked on them or were just mud banks if the paddy was wet.

After a few winding miles they reached the Licab River. On the far side was a screen of bamboo, and, passing through, they found themselves back on grasslands. Not far away was Lobong barrio. They halted just outside the collection of huts and linked up with Capt Joson's 100-man squadron. About 80 would escort the raiders. As the column departed at 1830 hours, the guerrillas fanned out on the

Pajota's Filipino guerrillas wore old US khakis, work clothes, and even Japanese uniform components. Their armament and web gear was just as varied. (US Army)

29

SCR-694 RADIO

There were no man-packed radios that could reliably transmit the required distances to allow the raiders to communicate directly with their distant base. The "six-niner-four" was a relatively new Signal Corps radio of modern design and would be the Rangers' lifeline. The set and its equipment weighed 108lb and were carried by three men in four canvas bags: radio transceiver, hand-cranked power generator, antenna components, generator tripod, and accessories (Morse code key, microphones, headset, etc). Accessories not required were left behind. It could not be operated on the move, but had to be set up with a long horizontal wire antenna strung between trees. The radio operated in the frequency range of 3,800 to 6,500 kHz in continuous wave (CW) radio telegraph and voice modes. Its voice range was approximately 15 miles and with CW Morse code the range was at least 30 miles. Further ranges could be achieved depending on atmospheric conditions and precise antenna length adjusted to the frequency and orientation. Power was provided by a GN-58A generator mounted on a folding tripod fitted with a seat. The operator turned a pair of hand-cranks. Spinning up the generator was not difficult, but as soon as the radioman began tapping the key the electromagnetic resistance in the generator coils made it extremely difficult to crank. (The pictured vibrator power unit, mounting, mast bracket and base were used only when fitted in a vehicle.)

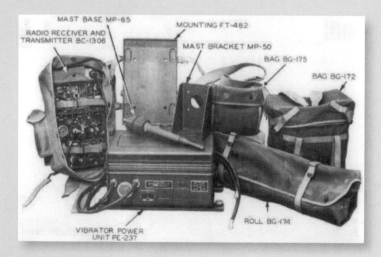

flanks and brought up the rear, with 20 remaining in Lobong to guard against Huks. Their route now took them through a forest.

The guerrillas were typically uniformed in worn military khakis or farmers' clothing, most with straw buri hats,[18] army fatigue caps, or M1917 steel helmets, while a mix of US web and Japanese leather gear was used. They were armed with a mix of .30cal M1903 Springfield and M1917 Enfield rifles with which the US Army, Philippine Scouts, and Philippine Army had been armed. Ammunition was generally plentiful owing to submarine deliveries, which also provided some M1 carbines, BARs, and Thompsons. Lapham had also received 50 M1 antitank mines, which the guerrillas had hidden for future use. They also carried Japanese 6.5mm or 7.7mm Arisaka rifles, and some 6.5mm Nambu light machine guns were also on hand. In some units only about one-third of the guerrillas carried firearms. The others were armed with bolo machetes (*itak*), which they had mastered as both a weapon and a

---

18 A wide-brimmed floppy hat woven from the fibers of the buri palm.

tool, and were intent on using to acquire a rifle. Unknown to the Rangers, the guerrillas also had four .30cal Browning M1917A1 water-cooled machine guns.[19] The fighters were mostly young men, few with previous military experience, but there were enough former Philippine Army, Philippine Scouts, and Constabulary to provide leadership and military skills. What the guerrillas lacked in practical experience they made up for in enthusiasm fired by their hatred of the Japanese.

Besides armed guerrillas, there were large numbers of auxiliaries of all ages and both genders, who did whatever was necessary to support the cause, serving as messengers, lookouts, guides, and medics. They hid supplies and materials, drove carts to transport men and equipment, provided food and water, purchased items on the black market for use by the guerrillas, gathered up useful materials left behind by Japanese units, treated the sick and wounded, collected and passed on information about the Japanese, painted patriotic slogans on walls, and kept an eye on neighbors collaborating with the Japanese, known as *Makapili*.

The Japanese allowed the Philippine Constabulary, the national police force, to remain active for local law enforcement. While some units conducted anti-guerrilla operations, most refrained from doing so or only went though the motions, alerting the guerrillas that they were about to launch an operation. Some units even held mock "battles" in the hills with the guerrillas in which the reported "dead" Constabulary members had in fact gone over to the guerrillas and their colleagues then requested

JANUARY 27
1945

1400 hours: Alamo Scouts set out for Guimba.

Ranger infiltration and exfiltration routes

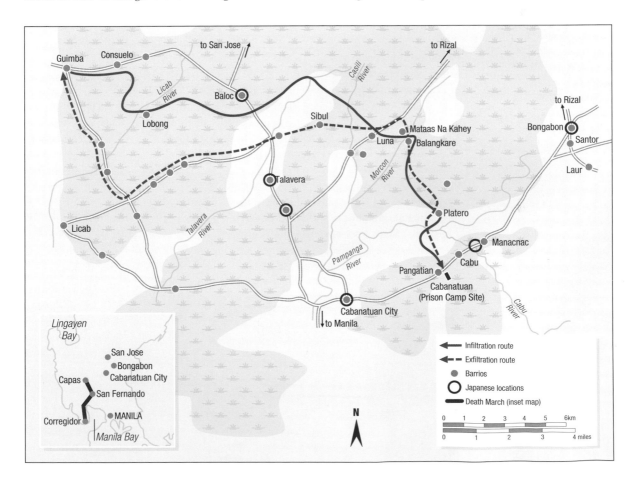

19 Two of the guns had been saved after the downfall and the other two captured from Huks the month before.

the Japanese replenish the ammunition they had "expended." Constabulary officers frequently passed intelligence to the guerrillas. As an example, 1st Lt Juanito Quitives, a Constabulary officer in Cabanatuan City, also commanded Squadron 200 of Lapham's Raiders, which would support the rescue. To complicate matters, many of the guerrillas did not speak English but rather Tagalog or related dialects, and Filipinos from different parts of Luzon could not always understand one another.

The column worked its way through 6 miles of forest in the growing darkness. They were emerging from the forest when the moon rose above the trees. The Rangers found themselves in an area of chest-high grass. Time was important, but Mucci had to conserve his troops' strength – they had a long approach and return march ahead of them. Skirting Baloc's south side, they cautiously approached Highway 5. In the moonlight they could see and hear the heavy traffic. It was mostly northbound and unending, and Mucci feared they might have to cross in ones and twos between vehicles. With some 200 troops crossing, there was a high risk of detection. He certainly did not want the force to be separated on opposite sides of the road and then detected: the remainder on the west side rushing the road and fighting their way across would result in high casualties, making it virtually impossible to complete the mission. A lone Japanese tank was spotted on the roadside guarding a bridge over a dry ravine. Using extreme stealth the raiders might be able to slip quietly under the bridge, follow the ravine to an area of high grass, and then make for a clump of trees a mile to the east – their rally point.

With hearts pounding, the men silently crept under the bridge one at a time. The four-man tank crew's conversation was never disturbed. Once all the men were accounted for, they pressed on eastward, paralleling the Talavera River a mile to their south. Reaching the shallow river about 3 miles east of the highway at 2400 hours, they crossed quickly, turned southeast, and, after 3 miles in the open, entered another forest. Extending their interval as they entered more open grassland, they experienced a mild scare, as muffled thumps sounded about them. Spreading out with weapons ready, the troops found the cause to be falling dead birds, for which no explanation was discovered. Their next obstacle was the Rizal Road, a branch road running from Highway 5 north of Cabanatuan City and angling northeast to Rizal, 7 miles up the road. The traffic was light with numerous breaks and tanks were sited at intervals of several hundred yards as mobile pillboxes. They crossed during gaps in traffic beginning at 0400 hours and again rallied among trees after dashing a mile through high grass. They next moved 1½ miles east, crossed the Morcon River, went on east for another mile, and then followed a winding route south avoiding villages and their barking dogs. They were almost at Balangkare, the rendezvous with the Alamo Scouts.

These guerrillas are armed with Springfield .30cal M1903 rifles, Japanese Arisake 6.5mm Type 38 (1905), rifles, and a Japanese Nambu 7.7mm Type 95 (1935) heavy machine gun. The horse was used to haul the machine gun. (US Army)

Pajota's guerrillas were armed with four of these Browning .30cal M1917A1 water-cooled heavy machine guns. They proved invaluable in halting the fanatical Japanese charges in their attempts to force the Cabu River bridge. The guns actually used by the guerrillas had brass water jacket front caps. (US Army)

As the Rangers made their approach march and the Scouts reconnoitered the camp, the guerrillas were mobilizing according to Lapham's instructions. Over a thousand guerrillas were marching on the objective area. They traveled in small groups or individually by foot, horse, and carabao cart, often taking misleading and out-of-the-way routes. Guerrillas seldom organize according to a fixed table of organization. They are recruited locally by respected leaders to whom they are loyal. Village and family ties are more important than conventional military structure. Lapham recognized this and organized the different bands into "squadrons." In US service a squadron is a battalion-sized unit, but Lapham designated them as such irrespective of strength, though most were of company-size. This also misled the enemy, who would have no idea of a particular unit's size.

Final planning

The Rangers halted outside Balangkare at 0600 hours, just over 2 miles north of Platero and 5 miles from the camp. In a clump of trees they linked up with Nellist and Rounsaville. The Scouts had been busy since their arrival, but they had not had time to accomplish all they had set out to do.

Breaking up into smaller teams, the Scouts had reconnoitered the trails between Balangkare and Platero, from the latter to the camp, along the Pampanga River, and traversed the entire area around the camp. They had not been able to approach too closely because of the open terrain. Additionally they collected a great deal of information from the guerrillas.

Mucci was disappointed by their report. They had been unable to scout Cabanatuan City owing to lack of time and because there were thousands of enemy troops around the city, guerrilla reports claiming an entire enemy division was present. There were at least 300 troops bivouacked near the Cabu River bridge a mile from the camp and there were still 200 resting troops in the camp along with the guards. Night-time vehicle and foot traffic on the road was unremitting. They could not accurately determine the number of guards, but the towers and fighting positions were each manned by two to four men. The fields around the camp were completely clear of vegetation. Coupled with the full moon, approaching the camp across hundreds of yards of bare ground was extremely risky. The good news was that the prisoners were

Participating guerrilla units

Unit	Commander	Strength
Commander	Capt Juan Pajota	
XO	Capt Luis De La Cruz	
HQ Company	1st Lt Florencio Bernardo	20
Squadron 200	1st Lt Juanito Quitives	100+
Squadron 201	1st Lt Jose Hipolito	430
Squadron 201A	1st Lt Ricardo Mendoza	100
Squadron 202	1st Lt Regino Bobila	100+
Squadron 203	1st Lt Veillariuman	115
Squadron 204	2nd Lt Bienvendo Erive	130
Squadron 210A		100
Squadron 211	1st Lt Toribio Paulino	36
Squadron 213	1st Lt Eduardo Joson	100

still there, were not being inordinately mistreated, and there appeared to be no preparations to move them. They also reported that the guerrillas were completely cooperative, although their estimates of enemy strength appeared exaggerated.

Mucci needed more detailed information on the camp. The aerial photograph, while valuable, provided only an overhead view, so ground-level reconnaissance was necessary. He wanted more information on the Japanese bivouacked at the bridge and laying over in the camp. Some reconnaissance would have to be accomplished in daylight in order to observe details. Due to the extent of the road traffic, Mucci was already considering postponing the raid until the next night. There was a danger that the situation could worsen: for example, road traffic might increase, more troops might arrive, or they might suddenly march the prisoners away.

While the meeting was under way, a young guerrilla arrived on a mule, introducing himself as Capt Juan Pajota. Lapham had previously recommended this guerrilla to Mucci and he was asked to sit in on the planning sessions. However, regardless of what had been discussed and without gleaning further information from Pajota, Mucci suddenly announced he intended to attack the camp after nightfall.

Pajota was reportedly stunned and questioned the decision. Risking Mucci's displeasure, Pajota announced that his own scouts were reporting to him hourly and that launching the mission at this point in time would be virtually suicidal. Almost a thousand more Japanese were moving toward the Cabu bridge from Bongabon and would arrive shortly. This was the 359th Battalion. With this substantial Japanese unit laying over in the camp it would clearly be a dangerous undertaking. Significantly, Pajota was able to provide more specific details on the camp itself, as he had been stationed there before the war. Moreover, while posing as civilians he and other guerrillas had been able to approach the camp and report on any major changes.

In addition, Pajota produced a very detailed hand-drawn map he had compiled and updated over the last three years. He pointed out the estimated Japanese troop strength at different locations and expressed his concerns about moving 500 weakened prisoners on foot cross-country. Pajota told Mucci that he had begun making arrangements for two-wheel carabao carts, an idea Mucci had not previously considered, and could also arrange for food from villagers on the return march.

Delaying the attack by one night would allow more intelligence to be collected, for more guerrillas to assemble, and for better arrangements to be made for support.

Mucci explained his initial plan of attack. Initially he foresaw only limited use of the guerrillas, but he would require them now owing to the increased number of Japanese troops in the immediate area. Ideally, a raiding force would be organized into three mutually supporting elements: (1) the attack force which would execute the mission: in this case, penetrate the camp, neutralize the guards, liberate the prisoners, and bring them out; (2) the support force providing suppressive and covering fire; and (3) the security force. This last was as important as the first two. The security force was typically organized into two or more elements to protect the rear and flanks of the attack force, warn of the approach of enemy forces, reinforce the attack force if the situation went bad, block or ambush enemy reinforcements, and cover the withdrawal of the attack force. The Rangers and Alamo Scouts together were too small a force to provide all three elements, so Mucci had no choice but to employ the guerrillas.

Since Mucci had no idea of how many guerrillas would be available, their quality, how well they were organized, or their armament, he could not make any realistic

**JANUARY 28
1945**

0715 hours: Rangers arrive at Guimba.

**JANUARY 28
1945**

1400 hours: Rangers begin their approach march.

Rangers en route to Cabanatuan POW Camp on January 29, 1944. They traveled very light, not even taking backpacks or sleeping gear. (US Army)

35

advance plans. Upon arrival at Balangkare he was only certain of Joson's 80 guerrillas that had accompanied him from Lobong. He asked Pajota how many armed guerrillas he had available in the immediate area. The Filipino reported he had 90 armed and 160 unarmed guerrillas in the Balangkare area.

Pajota was undertaking a common guerrilla leader's precaution. He answered truthfully in that he was asked how many men he had in the immediate area. Guerrilla leaders wisely never reveal their full strength and capabilities to anyone, even allies, and Pajota did not want to see his troops mis-utilized or exploited. While conventional commanders consider guerrillas to be an unknown quantity, guerrillas feel the same way toward conventional commanders. They first wish to learn more of the commander they are to work with, to determine his attitude toward the guerrillas – a reasonable fear of guerrillas being that a conventional commander might treat them as expendable and unimportant owing to their limited capabilities. Guerrilla commanders have another concern beyond the military, however. Their men are not just troops assigned to a unit – they are relatives, friends, and neighbors. Guerrilla commanders know their men's families and often attend the same schools and churches. They would have to live with them after the war and would be held accountable should things go awry.

Pajota was being cautious. He knew Mucci would want to use his guerrillas as blocking forces, but he wanted to learn more about Mucci's plan and how he intended to employ them before he committed more men. Mucci revealed that he planned to use Joson's squadron west of the camp to halt Japanese coming from Cabanatuan City and Pajota's men to block the Cabu bridge. This was rather a lean force to halt possibly over a thousand Japanese infantry with tanks, even if they had the benefit of the river gorge as an obstacle. The Japanese could easily out-flank them by crossing a few hundred yards on either flank and envelop them in short order – the odds of them holding out for more than an hour were slim. Mucci also wanted to use unarmed guerrillas to assist the prisoners as litter bearers, cart drivers, and messengers. To this end, Pajota offered more men – up to 400 – and promised that he could assemble numerous carts.

Another guerrilla leader ploy is never to reveal the guerillas' full capabilities, or limitations, in regards to armament, instead reporting that they do not have enough weapons and ammunition in the hope of receiving more. Pajota did not tell Mucci that he had four .30cal water-cooled machine guns, but was surprised to learn that the Rangers had not a single machine gun, only BARs. Mucci promised that he would reinforce Joson's roadblock with a bazooka team and that a bazooka would also be provided to the bridge-blocking force.

Pajota still did not reveal the full extent of his forces to Mucci, even though he now knew his mission. He wished to deploy them as he saw fit, having been over the ground and seen the Japanese positions himself. What he did not tell Mucci was that his Squadrons 200 and 202 – with just over 100 men each – would be held in reserve behind the roadblock. Squadrons 203 and 204 – with 115 and 130 men respectively – would be deployed behind the Japanese at the bridge and to the west of Manacnac and south of Highway 20.

Mucci's orders to Pajota were simple: deploy the blocking force west of the Cabu River bridge and, from 1930 hours, or when firing broke out, halt the enemy. The meeting continued with Mucci beginning to consider options, again including postponing for a day. The Scouts and guerrillas would soon be reporting more information. Arrangements were made for villages to feed the liberated prisoners, the rescue force, and the guerrillas. The Filipinos had little food because of Japanese rationing, but Mucci expected the advancing US forces to be able to provide food later. Carabao carts were to be collected and marshaled at designated points. Mucci also recommended that civilians be evacuated and stay off the highway. This would be done gradually, the civilians leaving one family at a time so as to not alert the Japanese.

Some of the Rangers taught the guerrillas how to operate the bazookas, while the rest caught up on sleep and guerrillas provided security. The cameramen were frustrated. They had taken few pictures and shot little film, so far everything of interest having taken place at night. It appeared that the real action of the raid would take place at night too.

In the meantime, the 359th Battalion had arrived at the Cabu bridge. It would have been better to have crossed the bridge before the unit bivouacked in case American aircraft blew it up during the day, but there was little concealment on the west bank. Among the trees on both sides of the road, Capt Oyanu discovered the remnants of four units, some 300 troops. They were without orders and planned to march east to Bongabon. One unit was a depleted tank company with four tanks and a truck armed with a machine gun. The tanks were about 300 yards from the bridge. They did not have enough fuel to make it to Bongabon, but they could reach Cabanatuan City. Oyanu absorbed the troops into his battalion and told their officers they would accompany him to Cabanatuan City to reinforce its defense. The tanks would be dug in. His force now numbered almost 1,200 troops. With most bivouacked in the trees paralleling the river north of the highway, and some on the south side along the highway for a short distance from the bridge, they settled in to sleep and wait out the day before marching into Cabanatuan

City that evening. A few more men of the Kinpeidan HQ from Cabanatuan City would arrive at the camp in the early morning. This would bring the strength of the unit in the camp to 210.

While Mucci was considering the overall operation, gathering intelligence, and coordinating with the guerrillas, he had tasked Capt Robert Prince to plan the attack on the camp itself, that is, taking out the sentries in the towers and fighting positions, suppressive fire, breaking into the camp, destroying the remaining guards and the resting unit, knocking out the tanks, collecting the prisoners, and getting them out of the camp. This last aspect he also coordinated with the guerrillas. They would have litter bearers ready to enter the camp on the heels of the Rangers. He strove to keep the plan as simple as possible. Prince's primary goal was to ensure there were as few friendly casualties as possible. The approach across exposed ground was dangerous enough, but to reduce the chance of alerting the Japanese he requested through the guerrillas that all chickens be cooped up and dogs muzzled and tied up or held indoors in Pangatian adjacent to the camp.

At 1600 hours, with sunset only two hours away, Mucci directed the radio team to transmit a message to the relay station at Guimba requesting that air cover on the planned withdrawal route be provided from 1900 hours. The message informed Sixth Army HQ that the mission was going as planned and that all was well. The Rangers and guerrillas formed up and began the 2½-mile hike to Platero, just over a mile

Capt Robert W. Prince, Commanding Officer, Company C, 6th Ranger Infantry Battalion, after the Cabanatuan raid. He was also the assault commander. Pistols were commonly carried in shoulder holsters in the Ranger battalion. (US Army)

37

JANUARY 29 1945

0600 hours: Rangers arrive at Balangkare, 5 miles from the camp.

north of the camp and bridge, and the final stopping place before the different elements broke up to take their positions.

After covering less than half a mile the Alamo Scouts arrived with new information. They confirmed that there were a thousand or more Japanese at the Cabu bridge, that at least 200 Japanese were in the camp, and that an estimated 7,000 were in and around Cabanatuan City. The enemy battalion at the bridge and the small available guerrilla blocking force to hold them changed Mucci's mind. He ordered the radio to be set up and sent another message, "New developments. 24-hour delay." The receipt of the message was acknowledged by the Guimba relay station and forwarded to Sixth Army HQ. Hearing the news, Krueger expressed concerns that he might have sent too small a force for the mission.

No doubt the troops were relieved. Word had spread about the arrival of the Japanese battalion. The column continued on to Platero and, much to their surprise, they entered the village with girls singing "God Bless America" and learned that a feast awaited them. The weary Rangers and Scouts were assigned in small groups to stay in houses as guests, where they could get a much needed night's rest. Guerrillas would secure the area. Some of the Alamo Scouts and guerrillas again reconnoitered the camp at 0300 hours, reporting no change and that traffic was still heavy on the highway.

Final preparations

On the morning of the 30th, the Americans were served a hearty breakfast and Mucci held a meeting with his officers and those of the Scouts and guerrillas. They had a full day to get ready, collect more intelligence, and refine their plan. To the Scouts he provided a list of information he required, while from Pajota he hoped to receive more information on the Japanese at the bridge. Mucci also wanted the guerrillas to show Prince the best route to the camp. At this point there were no changes to the overall plan. Capt Fisher, the battalion surgeon, linked up with the guerrillas' doctor and established a temporary field hospital in the Platero schoolhouse. Carabao carts were assembled on the banks of the Pampanga River near Platero, where food was collected and prepared for the expected prisoners. The 50 antitank mines were distributed as plans were finalized for the roadblocks. Pajota assigned 2nd Lt Anselmo San Padro with part of Squadron 201A to escort the Rangers to their attack position and serve as a reserve.

Time dragged by and the Scouts had not yet reported back. They had circumnavigated the camp three times and scouted the entire area. They were still unable to get close enough to the camp, especially the main gate, to obtain the detailed information Mucci needed. Across from the gate, however, was an abandoned nipa hut, so the Scouts sent word back to Platero to send two sets of Filipino clothes and hats. Donning the clothes, Lt Nellist and Pfc Rufo Vaquilar, a Filipino-American in his team, concealed their weapons and casually walked 600 yards up the highway. They traveled separately so the size difference between the 6ft American and the smaller Filipino-American would not be apparent to the guards. Reaching the compound, Vaquilar went almost to the gate, then walked across the field to the hut 350 yards from the gate. From there they had a good view of the camp using binoculars. As they were estimating ranges, making a sketch, and annotating the aerial photograph, much to their surprise, three more Scouts entered the hut. They had low-crawled almost 2 miles from the Pampanga River.

Nellist sent them back with the information that an increasingly impatient Mucci was awaiting, delivering it at 1430 hours. Rather than the usual four men per tower

JANUARY 29 1945

1600 hours: Mucci radios in request for air cover.

The approach

At 1700 hours, the Rangers, Scouts, and their accompanying guerrillas quietly departed Platero. They tied strips of white cloth around their upper left arms for identification. Staying behind was the radio team; the SCR-694 could not be operated on the move so it was better off in the village. They would send a success message based on the flares fired from the camp and have the radio packed up by the time the rescue force passed back through the barrio.

There were just over 370 men in the column that worked its way through bamboo and cogon grass to the Pampanga. They waded across where a sandbar divided the river into two streams and provided a knee-deep crossing; it was much deeper elsewhere. The column separated into three groups with the Rangers heading for the camp, Pajota's guerrillas toward the bridge to join those already there, and Joson's squadron to establish their western roadblock. They were accompanied by six Company F Rangers with bazookas. They were not too concerned with a threat from Cabanatuan City, as, with the telephone lines cut, the Japanese command could not be alerted. Even if they heard the firing from several miles away they probably would not respond – they were in a frontline area and unexplained gunfire was commonplace. Even if a relief force was dispatched, it would take time to assemble and it would move cautiously in the dark into an unknown situation. The Rangers and prisoners would be long gone by the time they reached the camp.

At first they pushed through high grass, but it soon gave way to rice paddies. The 30-man Company F platoon turned off to the east, heading for the stream they would follow under the highway to their support positions on the east and south sides of the camp. Company C continued toward the camp until they saw the silhouettes of its guard towers. The Rangers went to ground and waited – complete darkness was still over an hour away.

The guerrillas were cautiously moving into position along the river. HQ Company and Squadron 210A covered the bridge with a bazooka, a heavy machine gun, three BARs, and some Thompson guns. Their position gave them a line of sight east up the highway for 200 yards and the automatic weapons were set up so they could also

The Northorp P-61A Back Widow was a twin-engine, twin-tailboom, radar-equipped night fighter crewed by two men and armed with four 20mm cannons and four .50cal machine guns, all forward-firing. However, "Hard to Get" lacked the .50cal guns on its belly. (US Army)

The Filipino guerrilla movement was extremely successful and valuable for the liberation of the Philippines. Thousands of Filipinos joined the movement in a wide range of capacities. (US Army)

cover a wide frontage with overlapping fire. Bolo-armed guerrillas were behind them, ready to pick up the weapons of the fallen or carry off the wounded. They planted 25 antitank mines on the highway shoulders west of the bridge, an easy task since there were no Japanese sentries on the bridge, and the demolition charge was emplaced near the bridge's east end.

At 1830 hours, there was just one hour before the attack. The Japanese at the bridge were eating their evening meal and putting out their fires before dark fell. It would not be long before they were on the road to Cabanatuan City.

Pajota's guerrillas were either in position or awaiting full darkness to allow them to move in closer to the river. Joson's Squadron 213 and the Ranger bazooka team were occupying the roadblock west of the camp in a V-shaped ambush with the six Rangers on the south side of the highway and the guerrillas on the north. They too planted 25 mines on the highway shoulders west of the bridge, while Carabao carts were still assembling at the Pampanga River crossing.

The Company C Rangers were slowly low-crawling a half-mile across the dry rice paddies in the dimming light, their knees and elbows digging painfully into the hard soil and scattered carabao dung. Cautiously, they inched towards the objective, occasionally exposing themselves as they crawled over the intervening dikes. Lt Nellist in the hut north of the camp watched the Rangers snake forward. He and his comrade would soon shed their civilian clothes and join them.

Suddenly, a loud clanging reverberated from the camp. Every American and Filipino within hearing froze, holding their breath as they automatically pointed their weapons in the camp's direction. Yet the gates did not fly open, the guards did not take up firing positions, nor was there any sudden burst of activity.

The Rangers continued crawling, even more cautiously, while in the camp the prisoner who had just sounded "five bells," dropped the steel rod he had banged on a suspended pipe to indicate the watch change. The system had originally been implemented by sailors, but after so many months few POWs took the duty seriously.

In the distance the faint drone of an aircraft was heard. Despite the Rangers' concerns about the timely arrival of the distracting aircraft, the request had gone through the official channels surprisingly fast. The Sixth Army staff had sent the message Flash Priority and it arrived at the 459th Night Fighter Squadron, 86th Fighter Wing, Fifth Air Force at beach-side Lingayen Airfield just before 1700 hours. The squadron A2 (intelligence officer) alerted the CO and they read over the mission's requirements. They were also directed to dispatch additional aircraft to patrol the surrounding area and attack vehicles on the roads as well as to be prepared to support the Rangers if they should get into trouble.

The P-61A Black Widow crew of "Hard to Get" were selected for the diversionary mission simply because they were next in line on the mission board. The crews of these specialized hunter-killer aircraft were highly experienced and on average slightly older than most other fighter pilots. The A3 (operations officer) briefed the two flyers, pointing out the camp's location and telling them that they were to make low-level passes to distract the guards from the Rangers' approach. A Sixth Army captain would accompany them as an observer. They were also directed to attack any vehicles seen on the highway running in front of the camp. Other P-61s would be sent to hunt along nearby roads. They were to attack only vehicles and troop formations on roads, not personnel traveling off-road.

"Hard to Get" was airborne at 1725 hours and winging toward the camp 60 miles to the southeast. The fighter was flown by Capt Kenneth R. Schneber with 1st Lt Bonnie B. Rucks as the radar observer. Unfortunately, the Sixth Army observer's name is unknown. Two Black Widows already airborne were also diverted to Nueva Ecija Province to assist and seven more were soon sent aloft. Each was given a sector over Nueva Ecija and they were ready to engage any Japanese movement or replace "Hard to Get" if she developed mechanical problems.

"Hard to Get" turned broad circles over the area looking for landmarks. Dropping their altitude the crew made out the Cabu River, then the highway and bridge. At 1835 hours, the powerful engines screamed over the Japanese bivouac at 200ft, scattering startled troops, guards all but leaping from the towers as she roared over. So low was their approach that the flyers could see the Rangers lying prone in

Overleaf

1946 hours, Capt. Prince's red flare falls to the ground as S.Sgt Theodore Richardson of 1st Platoon, Co. C blasts the lock off the main gate with his .45, immediately after having it shot out of his hands and recovering it. S.Sgt James Millican, after literally cutting into the sentry in the guard post, turns his BAR on the guardhouse, which had been blasted by grenades. Another BAR man, Pfc Leland Provencher, shoots the sentry further down the road who had shot Richardson's pistol out of his hand. The two guards in tower are shredded by concentrated fire from most of 1st Platoon and fall to the ground below. The Rangers charge through the open gate into the POW camp.

Some freed prisoners were in such bad shape that they had to be spoon-fed in the homes of Filipinos while passing through the small barrios. The grateful Filipinos gladly shared what little food they had. (US Army)

the rice paddies. Throttling the aircraft back they climbed to 1,000ft and turned back to follow the highway over the bridge again. The men of the 359th Battalion knew better than to fire at the deadly black aircraft. "Hard to Get" came directly over the camp with the guards crouching in the towers and the prisoners, scrambling out of the barracks, waving wildly. Unbeknown to the flyers, the POWs were arguing – was the strange plane American or Japanese? They had never seen a plane of the likes of this one – futuristic looking and completely black in color with no insignia. One prisoner swore he saw a naked woman painted on the nose … it had to be American! The black plane wheeled and made repeated passes for a further 20 minutes.

By 1915 hours, Company F's 2nd Platoon had successfully crawled through the drainage ditch and stream paralleling the camp's east side, approximately 200 yards out. Reaching the south fence, some men crawled west through a ditch parallel with the fence to take up firing points covering the southeast tower, fighting positions, and rear gate. The men in the stream-bed on the east side crawled in closer to their targets. A sentry in the northeast tower suddenly shouldered his rifle, aiming toward the Rangers. Again, everyone froze until he finally lowered his rifle. Remarkably, he had apparently convinced himself that whatever he had seen was nothing of consequence. Each team that had been assigned a tower or fighting position was soon in place between 6 and 25 yards away. They were confident that the sudden burst of fire from their M1 rifles, BARs, and Thompsons would rip apart the sentries now engaged in quiet conversation and a shared cigarette. Sgt Joe Youngblood's team was responsible for the southeast corner tower, which still appeared empty. They would fire on it anyway, taking no chances of overlooking a sentry. It was also his duty to cut the escape hole through the perimeter fences.

North of the camp, Company C's 1st Platoon, the break-in force, was in a ditch immediately across the highway and taking aim at unsuspecting guards while the 2nd Platoon was in a drainage ditch 10 yards behind them. In the paddy another 10 yards to the rear was the reserve of cameramen, medics, and guerrillas. They were awaiting the first shot from Lt Murphy with the Company F platoon on the east and south sides of the camp. Meanwhile, guerrillas shimmied up nearby telephone poles and cut the lines.

By 1930 hours, the official start-time for the assault, Murphy had not yet fired. No doubt the former Notre Dame football quarterback felt some uncertainty. He wanted to confirm that huts to his rear were empty, even though reassured by guerrillas that they were. He also wanted to know for certain that each team was in position. He sent two men to check the huts and another back down the line to double-check the teams. His cautiousness is easy to understand – up to this point the mission had, against the odds, played out perfectly. Nonetheless, Mucci and Prince grew increasingly concerned with each passing minute.

Capt Pajota, on a slight rise behind Squadron 201A, looked back toward the camp, waiting for a red flare and flashing gunfire. He was well aware that if the Rangers waited too long the bridge demolition charge might explode before they opened fire.

At 1945 hours, Lt Murphy concentrated on aligning three points: the peephole of his M1 rifle's rear sight, the front blade sight, and the head of a Japanese soldier. He took a deep breath, released a little air, and gently squeezed the trigger. One of the most daring raids of World War II was now under way.

Liberation

An explosion of fire erupted from around the three sides of the camp. The sentries at the gates, in the towers, and in the fighting positions were immediately cut down. A dead soldier tumbled from the southeast tower, thought to be unoccupied – Sgt Youngblood's cautious orders proving to be well-founded. Rangers shifted their fire from their primary targets to already obliterated adjacent positions just to make sure. They continued to fire into the guard quarters as they rushed forward. The bamboo huts were easily shredded with tracers and grenades showered into the Japanese positions even though the majority of the guards were already dead. Youngblood's team began cutting a 15ft-wide opening through the fences as Prince fired a red flare from an M9 hand-projector.

Across from the front gate, 1st Platoon cut down the guards in less than half a minute and charged across the highway, firing and throwing grenades as they ran. SSgt Theodore Richardson was assigned to break open the gate. Rather than blasting the padlock with his Tommy gun he battered it with the gun's butt. Failing, he pulled his pistol to shoot the lock and a sentry rushing out of the guardhouse shot it out of his hand as a BAR man gunned down the sentry. Recovering the pistol undamaged, Richardson shot the lock off. As they threw the gate open a man ran toward them shouting "What's going on here?" The Rangers withheld fire thinking he was a prisoner, but he turned and shouted in Japanese. They quickly brought him down and fired into the guards' quarters. 1st Lt William O'Connell's 1st Platoon raced across the highway and through the gate within a minute of the start of the attack. The platoon rushed down the central street, firing into buildings and running shapes to the right, repeatedly emptying their weapons into the guards' quarters. The sheds containing the suspected tanks were 300 yards inside the camp. A bazooka team closed to within 50 yards and fired three rockets into them. Troops of the transiting Kinpeidan HQ who had been piling into two trucks were riddled with bullets and the trucks set aflame. As the headquarters troops rushed forward they were silhouetted by the burning sheds and made easy targets for the advancing Rangers.

The moment gunfire broke out at the camp, the guerrillas opened up with a rattling barrage into the Japanese bivouacs across the river from less than 300 yards. A cracking detonation burst from the bridge, too early for any Japanese to have started crossing. As the smoke and dust cleared it was seen that only a few feet of the bridge's east end was shattered. Pajota directed his automatic weapons to sight on the

THE ASSAULT ON THE CABANATUAN PRISON CAMP

JANUARY 30, 1945

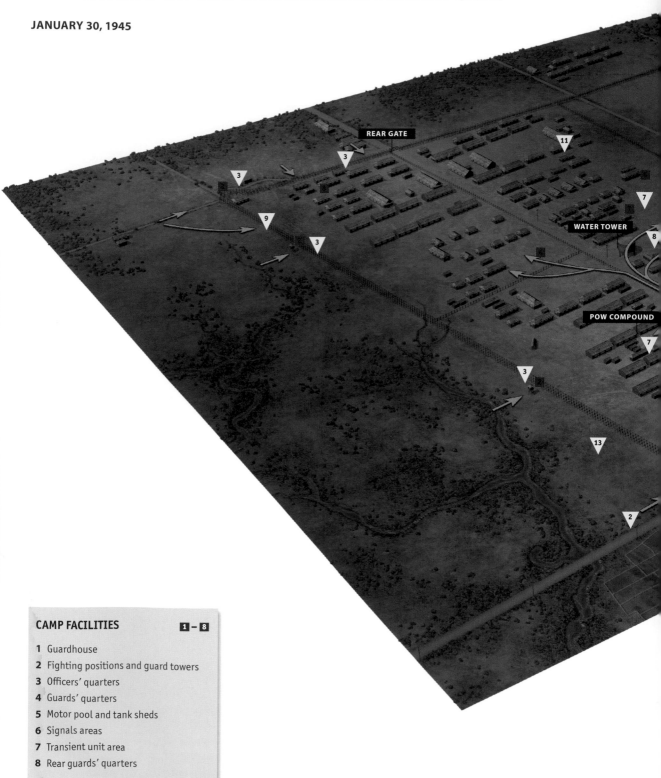

CAMP FACILITIES 1 – 8

1 Guardhouse
2 Fighting positions and guard towers
3 Officers' quarters
4 Guards' quarters
5 Motor pool and tank sheds
6 Signals areas
7 Transient unit area
8 Rear guards' quarters

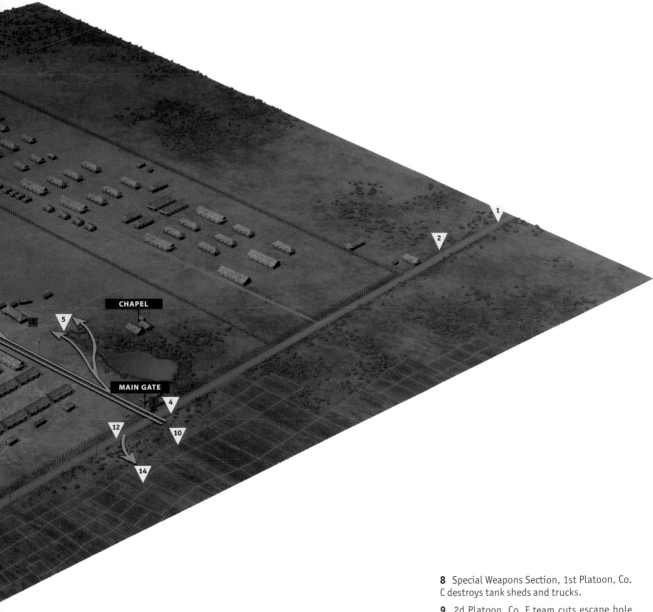

EVENTS

1 Squadrons 213 and 2d Platoon, Co. F establish a roadblock southwest of the camp.

2 Guerrillas cut telephone lines 150m east and west of the camp.

3 2d Platoon, Co. F fire support teams neutralize guard towers and fighting positions.

4 1st Platoon, Co. C neautralizes gate sentry and tower then breaks into main gate.

5 Men from 2d Section, 1st Platoon, Co. A split into two parties to attack both the officer and guards quarters

6 1st and Special Weapons Section, 1st Platoon, Co. C attacks tank sheds, signal area, and transient unit area.

7 1st and 2d Section, 2d Platoon, Co. C breaks into POW compound and attacks transient unit area.

8 Special Weapons Section, 1st Platoon, Co. C destroys tank sheds and trucks.

9 2d Platoon, Co. F team cuts escape hole through east fence.

10 POWs are ushered out of the compound and assemble outside of main gate.

11 Three grenade discharger rounds are fired onto highway.

12 Capt. Fisher and several men are wounded by grenade discharger rounds.

13 As 2d Platoon, Co. F fire support teams are withdrawn to highway, Cpl Sweezy is shot by mistake.

14 All raid forces and freed POWs are withdrawn to Pampanga River crossing and await the arrival of the buffalo carts.

bridge's end and any Japanese trying to jump the gap. The tanks, at least, could not cross and pursue the raiders. Less than five minutes into the attack, the first Japanese emerged from the trees, rushing the bridge unaware of the newly-formed gap. Streams of bullets tore into them as they attempted to leap across, and group after group charged only to be mowed down. The Japanese brought their machine-gun truck forward as additional support but this was quickly destroyed by some well-aimed bazooka fire, the survivors being picked off as they leapt clear.

At the camp, as the 2nd Platoon charged through the gate heading for the prisoner compound, there was complete pandemonium and confusion among the POWs. Some thought it was a guerrilla raid; others thought with horror that the Japanese were massacring them. Upon seeing Rangers in muddy green fatigues, field caps, strange boots, and carrying weapons they had never seen, they did not immediately know who they were. When they were captured, the army had worn khaki, but these men wore uniforms that looked frighteningly like the Japanese kit. Reportedly, the rescuers were shouting "we're Americans," "we're Yanks" and "we're Rangers," only to get responses like, "you don't look like Americans" and "what's a Ranger?" Some prisoners simply ran off and hid amidst the general confusion.

Rangers were forced to drag POWs out of their barracks, although more than 100 sick prisoners who had been housed in the hospital successfully made their own way to the main gate. But generally, Rangers had to keep prisoners moving by

Following their liberation, former POWs march to an Evacuation Hospital. (Corbis)

pushing and yelling "get the hell outa here!" As the situation sank home some prisoners began to shout in jubilation while others cried. Some had to be led out by hand as if they were children, many had to be carried. Tragically, Cpl James Herrick found a prisoner so weak he was unable to rise from his bunk. He picked up the man and carried him out, telling him that he was going home, despite the POW insisting: "leave me, I'm going to die." Outside, the man went limp – he had died of a heart attack just yards from the gate.

Fifteen minutes into the raid, the Rangers had not suffered any casualties. Rangers were still mopping up across from the prisoner compound and the reserve waiting in the ditch opposite the gate spread out along the highway in case of Japanese counterattacks. As Rangers and the POWs began moving down the highway, three mortar rounds impacted. These were fired from the far southeast corner of the camp and were probably 5cm grenade discharger (also known as "knee mortar") rounds. Company F Rangers in the rear opened fire on the trenches, silencing the discharger. Five men were wounded, including Lt Nellist and another Scout, but only one seriously. However, another Ranger was soon discovered with a severe stomach wound. The call went up for Capt Fisher, when it was suddenly realized that the wounded soldier was, in fact, the medical officer. Two Rangers and two guerrillas carried him to the Pampanga River crossing, as soldiers and POWs, many of the latter wearing only underwear, streamed out of the camp. There was a fear that prisoners would become separated in the confusion and that the weak might be left behind as the moon rose to light their return.

A half-hour into the battle, the Japanese at the bridge had all but given up. In all probability most of the officers were dead, having wasted themselves in futile rushes. Small groups continued to fire at the guerrillas only to draw more fire in return. Occasional grenade discharger rounds landed behind the guerrilla positions but this ceased once the guerrillas used their bazooka to fire on the tanks and supporting troops.

Northeast of Cabanatuan City, on the Rizal Road, which the raiders and their freed prisoners would have to cross later, a roving P-61 detected the 2nd Shusei Battalion dispatched to Cabanatuan City from San Jose. The Black Widow's three devastating passes ensured the battalion never reached its destination, with a total of 12 trucks and one tank destroyed.

Most of the prisoners had vacated the camp by 2010 hours. Rangers and guerrillas had to carry most, piggy-backing them or making hasty litters from rifles and shirts. It was 2 miles to the Pampanga River, where carts waited to take them to Platero to be treated, fed, and organized. Many were still in shock and had not yet fully understood that they were free.

Capt Prince and others made a final search of the compound as Mucci sent the groups on their way. Prince fired the second red flare, signaling for everyone to head to the Pampanga. Joson's roadblock would remain in place for a time, but the Rangers with him and a few guerrillas linked up with the main body to assist prisoners. Six Rangers from the camp's south side had not reported in and Prince waited with 20 men outside the gate.

At the Cabu River, the Japanese made little effort to continue their attacks. A small group attempted to cross the river further north and was wiped out. Pajota would remain in place until the third red flare arched into the sky.

Seeing the second flare, the six Rangers remaining on the south fence skirted the camp on its east side when bullets cracked over them. Judging it to be random fire from the bridge battle, they moved on and began to take scattered fire from inside the camp. Tragically, two bullets fired by a fellow Ranger struck Cpl Roy Sweezy in the chest, dropping him into a ditch, where he died as a medic worked on him. These

A former prisoner is assisted from an ambulance at the 92nd Evacuation Hospital. (US Army)

JANUARY 30 1945

1945 hours: The assault on the camp begins.

JANUARY 30 1945

2045–2145 hours: Rangers and POWs set out for Balangkare.

Rangers linked up with 1st Sgt Bosard on the highway, who was distressed to learn the company had lost a man and had had to leave his body behind.

At 2040 hours, Capt Prince was at the Pampanga River supervising the loading of stumbling prisoners into 25 carts as Rangers and prisoners trickled in and Fisher and the wounded Scout were treated in the field hospital. The rest of the Scouts established an ambush at the crossing site. At 2045 hours, one hour after the raid was launched, Prince fired the third red flare and departed for Balangkare. Joson withdrew his roadblock and, while Pajota was under no pressure from the Japanese and free to withdraw, he stayed in place until 2200 hours just to make sure. His squadrons circled to the southeast and around behind the Japanese to arrive at the Pampanga three hours later. The Filipinos were ecstatic – they had utterly destroyed a superior-strength Japanese battalion in their first stand-up battle. They came out of it with only a few men slightly wounded and all would be heroes.

Over 270 Japanese lay dead or dying in the smoldering camp; most of the wounded dying by dawn as no aid was forthcoming. Japanese bodies were literally stacked at the Cabu bridge and scores more littered the riverside woods. The 359th Battalion had ceased to exist. In the morning, battalion commander Capt Oyanu was still alive, but most of his officers were dead. Only 255 men of 1,200 survived and most were wounded.[21]

The loaded carabao carts were ordered on their way to Balangkare at 2145 hours. Meanwhile, the Filipino doctor and the Ranger medics were working frantically on Capt Fisher. As the column of prisoners departed north, Prince called the Alamo Scouts in from their ambush to guard the medical team and Fisher. A priest and a doctor, both freed POWs, stayed with them, along with Lts. Nellist and Rounsaville. Some of Pajota's men set up an ambush on the Pamganga River to stall any Japanese attempt to pursue the exfiltrating raiders.

The column closed on Balangkare at 2230 hours where 15 more carts joined them. The radio team there had difficulty establishing contact, but the long-awaited message was finally received at Guimba, where Sixth Army staff officers waited in apprehension, at 2300 hours. "BAKER ZULU GEORGE BAKER LEAVING SOME WITH FRIENDS" (BZ meant Mission Accomplished, GB meant Starting Back). Tech. 4 James Irvine, who had remained awake for nearly 60 hours awaiting this crucial message, was able to announce jubilantly to the expectant officers, "They've done it!"

They left Balangkare before midnight. Mucci was at the column's head with a limping Prince bringing up the rear. After almost 4 miles, they crossed the Morcon

---

21 Oyanu took his remaining men to Cabanatuan City the next day, passing the POW camp now infested with flocks of crows. They ran into the 1st Cavalry Division and, following this encounter, his remaining 70 men withdrew eastward, falling prey to guerrillas.

River and another mile brought them to Mataas Na Kahoy at 0200 hours, January 31. Here, 11 more carts waited as more prisoners weakened, and the convoy departed within half an hour of arriving. It was crucial that the column continued to move and some Rangers began taking Benzedrine to stay awake. The column stretched almost 2 miles, making it extremely vulnerable to attack as it snaked back towards Allied lines. Reaching the Rizal Road, they encountered an obstacle. The column could not cross directly as a steep bank barred the north side. They had to travel 1 mile southeast down the road to Luna before they could turn off. Roadblocks were established up and down the road during the transit, which took the strung-out column an hour. In the meantime, Capt Fisher was carried by six men to Balangkare, arriving at 0205 hours. There, a work detail cleared a light aircraft runway.

Reaching the Casili River the column halted for a rest at 0530 hours to allow stragglers to catch up. They received word that Huks in a village ahead would not allow them to pass. Negotiations were made via runners, but the Huks remained adamant. Mucci finally had enough and told the Huks they were all coming through and that he would level the barrio if there were any difficulties. The column passed through enduring nothing worse than hateful glares. At Sibul they received a more cordial welcome at 0800 hours in the form of food, water, and 19 more carts. With daylight and full bellies came the prisoners' realization that they were on their way home. This was evident in the smiling faces in the film footage taken that morning. At 0900 hours, Mucci learned via radio that Talavera, 12 miles closer than Guimba, was in American hands. He requested trucks for 412 personnel and ambulances for 100 to meet them on Highway 20 in two hours. Nearing the highway, aircraft were heard approaching and panicking prisoners clambered from carts. Four P-51 Mustangs roared over and put on an air show for the cheering men. Soon they met a 1st Battalion, 1st Infantry patrol and the trucks and ambulances arrived. They were trucked to Guimba where a jubilant reception awaited, with cheering GIs lining the roadside, and the 92nd Evacuation Hospital then took charge of them. Here Gen MacArthur would visit the liberated POWs as they convalesced on February 1.

Back in Balangkare, Capt Fisher died at noon, the requested plane never having arrived. He was buried there and the small group, harassed by Huks, made its way to Talavera, arriving in the evening where they found sleeping Rangers. Cpl Roy Sweezy's body was subsequently recovered from the camp by guerrillas on January 31, and he was buried alongside Captain Fisher.

JANUARY 30 1945

2300 hours: Mission success message radioed back to Sixth Army at Guimba.

The first leg of the trip home for the former prisoners. Cargo trucks depart the 92nd Evacuation Hospital headed for an airfield and then a sea voyage back to the States. (US Army)

ANALYSIS

The exhausted Rangers were quickly returned to Calasio and granted a well-deserved rest. News of the mission was publicly released on February 2. The unit continued to conduct company-size reconnaissance patrols and economy-of-force operations in support of the 6th Infantry Division and guarded Sixth Army HQ. One company was attached to the 37th Infantry Division for its final run up the west coast of Luzon to cut off retreating Japanese. In April and May, Rangers with sufficient time overseas were rotated home. This included some of the Cabanatuan veterans. More replacements arrived in July and, by September, most of the remaining veterans went home. The battalion was to have participated in the invasion of Japan and some veterans accompanied the battalion to Japan, where they guarded Sixth Army HQ and escorted sensitive item shipments. The Alamo Scouts served as Gen Krueger's bodyguards, while the Rangers made their new home in Fushimi Barracks outside of Kyoto and renamed it Camp Fisher. The battalion was deactivated there on December 30, 1945, the Alamo Scouts having been dissolved in November. Incredibly, the Scouts never lost a single man in the course of their 106 missions.

The Cabanatuan raid has gone down in the annals of US military history as one of the most perfectly planned and executed special-operations raids. According to Gen MacArthur, the Cabanatuan raid was "magnificent and reflects extraordinary credit on all concerned." The Sixth Army G2 weekly intelligence summary declared it "an almost perfect example of prior reconnaissance and planning." Few operations have since matched its success. Coincidentally, one of the few raids that did measure up to its standard was conducted just 24 days later, the Los Baños Internment Camp liberation by elements of the 11th Airborne Division under the control of the Eighth Army. Interestingly there was no mechanism or time for the Los Baños planners or raiders to have learned anything from Cabanatuan.

Effective "prior reconnaissance and planning" were the keys to the success of this operation, but there were other factors. One of the most important was the existence of the G2 Special Intelligence Subsection. It provided a specialized planning and coordination element with direct access to the G2, G3 (operations), and the Sixth Army commander. It was through this element that mission tasking, coordination, and control of the Rangers, Alamo Scouts, and guerrillas in the Sixth Army area were

Alamo Scout members of Nellist and Rounsaville Teams after the Cabanatuan POW Camp raid. (Left to right top row) Pfc Gilbert Cox, Pfc Wilbur Wismer, Sgt Harold Hard, Pfc Andrew Smith, and Pfc Francis Laquier. (Left to right bottom row) Pfc Galen Kittleson, Pfc Rufo Vaquilar, 1st Lt William Nellist, 1st Lt Thomas Rounsaville, and Pfc Franklin Fox. Not pictured are 1st Lt John Dove, Pfc Thomas Siason, Pfc Sabas Asis, and Pfc Alfred Alfonso. (US Army)

conducted. Today this might be called a "special operations forces infusion cell" or similar, but it is to Gen Krueger's credit that he formed such an element, while many similar commands lacked an equivalent. Unity of command is essential: an ad hoc assemblage of mixed forces seldom works. A specialized element familiar with the capabilities and limitations of special-operations units, and with immediate access to the highest commanders and staffs is critical for their effective employment. It is also necessary to ensure timely planning, coordination of support, and the launching of forces in order to accomplish rapidly emerging missions – there is no time for traditional, cumbersome, and conventional staff planning. It is also to Krueger's credit that he had the foresight to preserve the Rangers as a force to be committed to such missions rather than assigning them tasks that could be performed by conventional infantry. That said, two Ranger companies had been detailed to guard a radar station on a remote island, but this was the exception rather than the rule.

Flexibility and imagination were additional keys to success. The utilization of the Alamo Scouts – a dedicated specialized reconnaissance unit – to go in early, collect information, and then link up and work directly with the Rangers, was almost unprecedented and has only infrequently been repeated. Covert reconnaissance units and aggressive strike units require two entirely different types of special soldiers, psychological outlooks, and skill sets. While there are benefits in the strike unit controlling its own reconnaissance element, it may not always be the best choice.

Imagination was demonstrated in several ways: by incorporating the guerrillas and the support their auxiliaries provided to the operation, the good judgment to postpone the operation one day to collect more information, employing the Black Widow to distract the guards, detailing Rangers to reinforce guerrillas with bazookas, and the ability to quickly exploit late-arriving intelligence.

There were several external factors contributing to the success of the operation. If the terrain had been more difficult, either hilly, mountainous, swampy, or densely forested, it could not have been executed in time owing to prolonged travel time, and it might well have proved fatal to many prisoners. The Japanese were disorganized and command and control was breaking down as they were already under heavy American pressure, with some units withdrawing and others repositioning. Moreover, the replacement guards at the camp did not appear to be familiar with camp security and may not have been trained to counter an external threat. The original guards would have been more alert for a guerrilla attack or possibly put up a stiffer defense. Fortunately, the Japanese had little ability or inclination to pursue and had lost all pretense of air superiority. Certainly, if the Japanese had had effective air cover the outcome could have been very different.

Last, but not least, was the immeasurable value of the guerrillas. The operation simply would not have succeeded were it not for their contribution and sacrifice. Their skill at blocking and destroying the 359th Battalion made all the difference. The west roadblock, the rearguards, and the escorting of the prisoners were also valuable contributions. Just as crucial were the runners, scouts, guides, and medical assistance, to say nothing of the many carabao carts, litter bearers, and the food and water they supplied. The contribution of over a thousand guerrillas as well as that of perhaps thousands more civilians cannot be undervalued.

In hindsight, it is easy to find fault with the plans and execution of any mission. Few can be found with this operation. One potential problem was the use of a single radio operator manning the critical primary relay station outside of Guimba, a man who went for some 60 hours without sleep. He lacked relief and security, although there were probably some guerrillas present. This is especially curious as five men manned the secondary Ranger relay site. Another communication issue was the lack of an

Overleaf

The ancient carabaao cart was the principal means of transportation in rural Philippines. The 106 carts furnished by local villagers were instrumental to the safe evacuation of the former prisoners, with each cart carrying either four or five men. The simple straw-lined carts driven by mere boys were just as essential to the success of the operation as were weapons and radios. The exfiltration of the approximately 130 Rangers, Alamo Scouts and attachments; over 500 liberated prisoners, and a couple hundred guerrillas and auxiliaries was the most dangerous phase of the rescue. There was the risk of Japanese pursuit, engagement, even if by chance, with an unexpected enemy unit on the route home. This artwork shows the moment when four P-51 Mustangs roured overhead when the column was approaching Highway 5 on the morning of January 31. Rangers, liberated prisoners, and guerrillas cheered during the impromptu air show. Many guerrillas wore components of US and Japanese uniforms, but most wore civilian clothing to blend in better. The guerrilla illustrated carries the common .30cal M1917 Enfield with which the Philippine Army had been armed. The Ranger is armed with a .45cal Thompson M1 submachine gun.

1st Lt John F. Murphy of 2nd Platoon, Company F, (foreground, center) and other Rangers following the successful raid on Cabanatuan. (Corbis)

air-to-ground radio. There were small air liaison parties available with man-portable air-to-ground radios. This would have been especially valuable if the column had been mistakenly attacked by friendly aircraft or if the Japanese had pursued them.

To attain more mobile fire support Mucci replaced the assault sections' tripod-mounted M1919A4 machine guns with BARs. The BAR is suitable for maneuvering with a squad providing its base of fire, but as its 20-round magazine required constant changing it made a poor sustained fire-support weapon. Although BARs proved adequate under the circumstances, the situation could have demanded a weapon offering more firepower. Mucci might have been better off to have retained some M1919A4 Brownings for optional use. If nothing else they could have reinforced the roadblocks and proved invaluable if the Japanese had attacked the withdrawing column.

The Filipinos provided 106 carabao carts with drivers, each drawn by a single carabao (water buffalo). These were indispensable for carrying hundreds of disabled, weak, and ill prisoners. (US Army)

A final precaution that could have been taken would have been to deploy one of the remaining Ranger companies at an intermediate point on the return route. They could reinforce the column if attacked, counterattack pursuers from a flank, or, at the least, assist with the transport of prisoners.

No lengthy analysis is necessary to determine if the main goal was achieved: Allied prisoners in dire physical condition were rescued and protected from further harm. Operationally, a major unforeseen benefit was also achieved, with two infantry battalions and a Kempeitai headquarters unit utterly destroyed, further reducing resistance on the road to Manila.

CONCLUSION

Officially, 516 prisoners were released. However, the total includes a few more. The accompanying list is said to be accurate. Apparently the non-American civilians and the American who died of a heart attack in the camp were not included in the official total. Two American rescuers died and seven were wounded, one seriously. Miraculously only 12 guerrillas were slightly wounded. The feared retaliation on Filipinos did not materialize, as the Japanese were in retreat from the area within a day or two.

Liberated prisoners	
US Army	424
US Navy	38
US Marine Corps	2
British Army	20
Royal Navy	2
Royal Dutch Army	3
US civilians	28
Norwegian civilians	2
Canadian civilian	1
British civilian	1
Filipino civilian	1
Total	**522**

Gen MacArthur awarded Mucci the Distinguished Service Cross (the highest medal for valor after the Medal of Honor). All other officers received the Silver Star and the enlisted men the Bronze Star. The awards were presented by Gen Krueger on March 3 at Sixth Army HQ in San Jose. Company C and 2nd Platoon, Company F and attached personnel received the Presidential Unit Citation, a decoration considered equivalent to the Distinguished Service Cross for an individual. The battalion as a whole was later awarded the Philippine Presidential Unit Citation. All participating Filipino guerrillas were presented with the Bronze Star in 1947.

Besides Mucci's promotion to full colonel, Capt Prince was promoted to major. He took over command of the 6th Ranger Battalion in July 1945 and closed the unit out. Most officers involved in the raid left the army after the war. Lt Nellist, however, made the army a career, retiring as a colonel. A number of enlisted men also became career soldiers with some eventually serving in Special Forces.

One other individual should be mentioned – Japanese LtCol Mori Shigeji, the former commander of Cabanatuan POW Camp. He had departed days before the raid with the other original guards, but was nonetheless sentenced to life imprisonment with hard labor for mistreating prisoners.

Today, nothing remains of the Cabanatuan POW Camp except six concrete foundation blocks for the water tower. The Cabanatuan POW Camp Memorial, with two walls listing the names of the 3,000 POWs who died there, was dedicated in 1982 by the Defenders of Bataan and Corregidor Foundation. The memorial, near the camp's center with the water tower blocks framing its entrance, is maintained by the US Battlesites Commission. The remains of POWs in the camp cemetery were

The former Cabanatuan prisoners arrive at 6th Infantry Division lines, January 31, 1945. Many wore only underwear as they had to depart so fast. (US Army)

61

Besides food, water, and emergency medical treatment, a critical order of business was to compile a roster of the freed prisoners along with all personal data as we can see the soldier on the left doing. (US Army)

disinterred and reburied in the Manila American War Cemetery. An even more impressive memorial to the raiders and guerrillas is a massive sundial depicting the raid's events, maintained by the provincial government. Outside this is a small memorial for the prisoners dedicated in 2003 and maintained by the Philippine National Historical Institute. There is also a small memorial listing the 176 West Point graduates who died in the camp. A small memorial honoring Capt James Fisher is located in Balangkare and appropriately serves as a rice-drying platform. The E.L. Joson Memorial Hospital in Cabanatuan City commemorates the guerrilla leader.[22]

The Cabu River bridge was replaced by a steel girder bridge in 1950. The small communities have grown vastly since the war and National Highway 20 is mostly lined with houses and businesses. Most areas along the infiltration and exfiltration routes are still cultivated, and have likewise expanded, covering many of the former grasslands and forests.

A motion picture, *The Great Raid*, was released in 2005 on the 60th anniversary of VJ-Day[23] and adapted from the book *The Great Raid on Cabanatuan*. While the movie portrayed the raid reasonably well, there were factual errors. Many of the Rangers and Alamo Scouts were given fictitious names (Scout Lieutenants Nellist and Rounsaville, for example). A twin-engine Lockheed Hudson was used rather than a P-61, as none of the four surviving Black Widows were flyable. The camp was shown well lit with electric lights, but in reality there were few. The movie depicted Kempeitai military police taking over the camp to execute the prisoners; neither this nor the execution of 12 Cabanatuan prisoners occurred. The Kinpeidan HQ was a Kempeitai unit, but was merely passing through. As it was filmed in Queensland, Australia, the oak and pine trees were out of place. To the movie's credit, however, the guerrillas were adequately acknowledged.

22 Eduardo Joson was the governor of Nueva Ecija Province from 1959 to 1992, making him the longest-serving politician in the Philippines.

23 *The Great Raid* was filmed in 2002, but its 2003 release was postponed because it was felt the prisoner execution scenes were inappropriate following the recent Islamic terrorist hostage beheadings. Contributing to the delay was a split between the two production companies. Steven Spielberg planned to produce his own movie on the raid to be titled *Ghost Soldiers* and based on the book of that name, but the project was dropped in 2003.

BIBLIOGRAPHY

Alexander, Larry. *Shadows in the Jungle: The Alamo Scouts Behind Japanese Lines in World War II*. New York: New American Library, 2009

Breuer, William B. *The Great Raid on Cabanatuan: Rescuing the Doomed Ghosts of Bataan and Corregidor*. Hoboken, NJ: John Wiley & Sons, 1994

Johnson, Forrest B. *Hour of Redemption: The Ranger Raid on Cabanatuan*. New York: Manor Books, 1978

King, Michael J., Jr. *Rangers: Selected Operations in World War II*. Leavenworth Papers No. 11. Ft Leavenworth, KS: Combat Studies Institute, 1985

Lapham, Robert and Norling, Bernard. *Lapham's Raiders: Guerrillas in the Philippines, 1942–1945*. Lexington: University Press of Kentucky, 1996

Knox, Donald. *Death March: The Survivors of Bataan*. Fort Washington, PA: Harvest Books, 2002

Rottman, Gordon L. *World War II Pacific Island Guide: A Geo-Military Study*. Westport, CT: Greenwood Publishing, 2001

Sasser, Charles W. *Raider*. New York: ST. Martin's Griffin, 2006

Sides, Hampton. *Ghost Soldiers: The Epic Account of World War II's Greatest Rescue Mission*. New York: Anchor Books, 2002

Smith, Robert R. *United States Army in World War II: Triumph in the Philippines*. Washington, DC: US Government Printing Office, 1963

Zedric, Lance Q. *Silent Warriors of World War II: The Alamo Scouts Behind Japanese Lines*. New York: Pathfinder, 1995

President Roosevelt meeting 12 of the veterans from the raid on Cabanatuan. (Corbis)

INDEX

References to illustrations are shown in **bold**.